I'LL NEVER FORGET

My First Car

I'LL NEVER FORGET MY FIRST CAR

STORIES FROM BEHIND THE WHEEL

Bill Sherk

Copy-Editor: Andrea Pruss
Interior and Cover Design: Andrew Roberts
Printer: Transcontinental

Library and Archives Canada Cataloguing in Publication

Sherk, Bill, 1942-
   I'll never forget my first car : stories from behind
the wheel / Bill Sherk.

ISBN-10: 1-55002-550-3
ISBN-13: 978-1-55002-550-7

   1. Automobiles--Humor. 2. Automobiles--Anecdotes.
I. Title.

TL162.S53 2005   C818'.602   C2005-900940-3

1   2   3   4   5   09   08   07   06   05

Conseil des Arts du Canada   Canada Council for the Arts   Canadä   ONTARIO ARTS COUNCIL
CONSEIL DES ARTS DE L'ONTARIO

We acknowledge the support of the Canada Council for the Arts and the Ontario Arts Council for our publishing program. We also acknowledge the financial support of the Government of Canada through the Book Publishing Industry Development Program and The Association for the Export of Canadian Books, and the Government of Ontario through the Ontario Book Publishers Tax Credit program, and the Ontario Media Development Corporation.

Care has been taken to trace the ownership of copyright material used in this book. The author and the publisher welcome any information enabling them to rectify any references or credit in subsequent editions.

J. Kirk Howard, President

Cover photo courtesy of Frank T. Sherk
Back cover photo courtesy of Harry Weale
Author photo courtesy Jim Domm

Printed and bound in Canada.
Printed on recycled paper.

www.dundurn.com

Dundurn Press	Gazelle Book Services Limited	Dundurn Press
8 Market Street, Suite 200	White Cross Mills	2250 Military Road
Toronto, Ontario, Canada	Hightown, Lancaster, England	Tonawanda NY
M5E 1M6	LA1 4X5	U.S.A. 14150

I'LL NEVER FORGET

My First Car

This book is dedicated to the person or persons unknown who purchased my 1940 Mercury convertible when it was new, followed by:

1951 — Junior Ritchie
1955 — Jim Robinson
1956 — Bursel Nead
1956 — Neil Nead
1957 — Dick Garant
1958 — Cliff Garant
1959 — Bill Sherk
1962 — Marshall Morgan
1964 — John Martin
1965 — Bob Fielder
1966 — Ted Carleton
c. 1975 — Dennis Smith
c. 1976 — Roy Solmes
c. 1977 — Bill Parm
c. 1980 — Laverne Allair
2001 — Bill Sherk again!
2003 — Scott Wood, who still owns the car today.

Table of Contents

INTRODUCTION

Remember your first car? Of course you do. Chances are it was an old clunker with lots of things wrong with it. But at least it ran, and it got you moving into the adult world.

Or did it? My first car (see page 11) was a 1940 Mercury convertible that I purchased for $150 on June 8, 1959. It had no engine and no transmission, and I had to push it home using my mother's 1957 Buick Century four-door hardtop. The Merc had been lowered, and the front bumper of the Buick kept riding over the rear bumper of the Merc and banging into the trunk lid as I pushed it home along Talbot Street West in my hometown of Leamington, Ontario. The local Studebaker dealer, Gerald Scratch, steered the Merc. The dents I put in the trunk lid that day were still on the car when I re-purchased it forty-one years later.

In a recent interview I had on CBC Radio in Toronto, a listener phoned in to tell us his first car was a 1936 Chevy four-door sedan. It ran reasonably well, but he discovered after buying it that the engine block was cracked and water was leaking out onto the road. He couldn't afford to have the crack repaired, so he mounted a ten-gallon drum full of water on the roof and ran a pipe from the drum to the top of the rad. The pipe (with a faucet) went past the driver's window, and whenever he noticed the rad overheating, he reached out — while he was driving! — and added a couple of gallons without even slowing down.

Bob Carpenter's first car was a 1932 Pontiac four-door sedan that he purchased in his hometown of Simcoe, Ontario, in the early 1950s. He couldn't get it running, but he drove it anyway; he was able to perform this miraculous feat because a friend who drove a service truck for a local gas station towed Bob free of charge all over the countryside behind the wheel of his first car. They did this many times, and Bob often invited friends to come along for the ride while he "drove" his car.

Most people drove someone else's car before they bought their own first car. Marty Gervais of the *Windsor Star* will never forget his first time behind the wheel. "I never learned to drive a car until I was twenty-two. I was in an Austin-Healey Sprite with my wife — or soon-to-be wife — and we were headed to Toronto. She was tired and asked if I wouldn't mind driving. I had never been behind the wheel of a car until that moment but thought I could fake it. That proved to be impossible. I sat there staring at the lit-up dashboard controls.

"I guess it was a macho thing on my part, and I didn't want to admit to not being able to drive. You see, when I was growing up, driving was a rite of passage, like puberty. Somehow I missed that stage. Driving a car, that is.

"Thus began my education behind the wheel of a car. On the 401. At night. In sleet. With meticulous and patient instruction from my wife. (Such instructions continue to this day, of course.) The rest is history. A string of speeding tickets and running amber lights — my specialties."

And so it goes. Every car has a story to tell, and every motorist does too. This book contains over fifty "auto" biographies collected from across Canada.

Thousands of similar stories have yet to be published. If you would like to see the story of your first car (or your favourite car) in my next book, please turn to page 183.

Bill Sherk
Leamington, Ontario
March 15, 2005

I'LL NEVER FORGET MY FIRST CAR

The janitor at the Leamington high school owned it, and I eyeballed it for a whole year before I bought it. I didn't have the $600 he wanted for it, so I polished cars in my spare time (I was still in school) and saved my money, hoping I would have enough before he sold it to someone else. It was a tomato red 1940 Mercury convertible, nosed and decked and lowered with air scoops in the hood, running boards, push-button door handles, a 1949 Ford push-button radio, 1948 Chrysler "flip-flop" window cranks, red plaid slipcovers on the front seat, a 1948 Ford steering wheel, one Kaiser wheel disc, a gaping hole where the rear window used to be, three white-wall tires, and a bullet hole through the roof. I had to have it.

Under the 1940 hood was a 1951 Studebaker overhead valve V8 engine — seven hundred pounds of horsepower and much heavier than the original flathead V8.

Cliff Garant was the owner. He wanted to get rid of it, and he came up with a plan that reeled me in. He removed the 1951 Studebaker engine and transmission and put them into a

Here I am at seventeen in the summer of 1959 just after buying my first car — a 1940 Mercury convertible with no engine. Air scoops had been cut in the hood when Jim Robinson rebuilt the car in 1955. The rush of air through those scoops blew the hood right off the car when I test drove it in the summer of 1960.

1951 Studebaker four-door sedan, which then became his family car. Now I could buy his 1940 Mercury convertible for only $150, and it was missing only two parts — the engine and transmission.

It was Monday, June 8, 1959, and I couldn't get to the bank fast enough (the CIBC on Talbot Street East in downtown Leamington). I had borrowed my mom's 1957 Buick Century four-door hardtop that morning, but I didn't tell her or my dad what I was up to.

My mother had threatened to throw me out of the house a year ealier when I had tried to buy another 1940 Mercury convertible in Toronto. I had backed out of that deal, but now I was a year older (seventeen) and figured this time I could pull it off and still live at home.

As soon as I emerged from the bank with the money for the car, I realized I had forgotten to bring someone else along to help me push the car home. Just then, I bumped into Gerald Scratch, the local Studebaker dealer, who had a beautiful 1913 Studebaker touring parked in his showroom. Surely he would be sympathetic to a young fellow buying an old car. He was. He agreed to steer the Merc while I pushed it with Mom's Buick. We found the Merc parked in the mud behind the high school football field. The engine and transmission were now gone. The radio and battery were gone too.

With the battery gone, the push-button door handles no longer worked. I reached in through the window to open the driver's door for Mr. Scratch, and he slid behind the wheel. That's when I noticed the steering column was attached to the dashboard with a wire coat hanger. "Take it slow and we'll be all right," he said.

I began pushing from behind with the Buick — a little too fast at first. The front bumper of the Buick rode up over the low rear bumper of the Merc and put a good-sized dent in the trunk lid. (That same dent was still there when I bought the car for the second time forty-one years later.)

Finally we got moving. For a car with no engine, the Merc made a horrendous racket. We stopped and discovered the non-original open driveshaft was still connected to the rear end, and the rear wheels were making it roll around inside the frame. It sounded louder than a freight train as we headed down Elliott Street, then west along Talbot Street toward my home on Armstrong Drive. My mother could hear the noise from five blocks away but didn't know what it was. Our driveway wrapped around the back of the house, and imagine my mother's shock as she looked out the kitchen window and saw an old, beat-up, tomato red car making this awful racket while rolling into the backyard, steered by an elderly gentleman she had

Dennis Smith snapped this photo around 1975 when he found (and bought) my car on a turkey farm near Perkinsfield, Ontario. He gave me this photo in 1993. According to the licence plate, the car had been off the road since 1966.

never seen before. Then she saw her own car with me behind the wheel, pushing this ancient wreck to a standstill behind our beautiful Cape Cod colonial home.

My mom was not amused, and neither was my dad when he came home for lunch. He told me I was too young to have a car of my own, and he drove me over to Cliff Garant's house at 38 Churchill Avenue to have him take back the car and return my money. My heart was in my mouth as we knocked on Cliff's front door. But Cliff came through for me with flying colours. He told my dad he had already spent the money from the sale to pay his property taxes, and furthermore he would like to talk to his lawyer.

Dad and I drove home and waited by the phone. We didn't have to wait long. Cliff called to say his lawyer had told him the deal was legal, and then he said the words I'll never forget: "Bill, it looks like you've bought yourself a car."

I repeated this to my dad. A long silence followed, then he said, "Well, I guess you may as well keep it. You wash it and get it all shined up and I'll get my camera and we'll take some pictures of it." That still warms my heart after all these years, and I still have those pictures. Later that summer, just after I got the car running and back on the road, I parked the Merc across the road from our house, and my dad took the picture you now see on the front cover of this book.

Finding an engine for my 1940 Mercury was not easy. The frame had been butchered to install the 1951 Studebaker engine a year or two earlier, and I didn't want that set-up anyway. Not enough horsepower. I wanted an engine that could rip the asphalt right off the road. Dick Garant (Cliff's brother and another previous owner of the car) suggested I phone Remington Auto Wreckers on Howard Avenue in Windsor to see if they had one of the hot late-model small-block Chevy V8 engines. They did. A 1957 Chevy Bel Air four-door sedan had rolled

My good friend Kent Weale snapped this photo in Peter Clancy's driveway in Port Credit, Ontario, in October 1961. By this time I had repainted the Merc from tomato red to tough-looking black primer (a.k.a. California suede). I frequently drove my car around Toronto with the front fenders off, and the police never pulled me over.

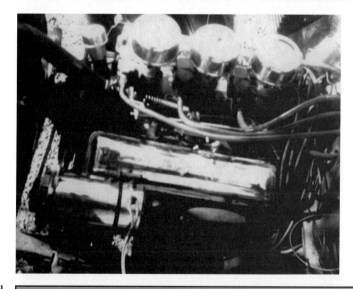

Kent Weale snapped this photo of the 1957 Chevy 283 V8 the same day. Before he could give me the photo, we lost touch with one another. We became friends again in 1993, when he gave me this and the previous photo thirty-two years after taking them.

over in an accident, but the engine was okay. It was a 283-cubic-inch V8 and I could have it for $300. I was a little uneasy about buying an engine that cost twice as much as my entire car, but there was no turning back now. I turned my wallet upside down and bought it while thinking, *Before I'm finished, this old car will take a vacuum cleaner to my bank account.*

Found at last! Kent Weale and I pose with the remnants of my first car on January 2, 1994, in a garage in Rednersville, Ontario, after a six-year search.

Next on my list was a transmission. I couldn't use the automatic transmission from Remington's Chevy. Back in the 1950s, if you put an automatic transmission into a hot rod, everyone would laugh you right out of town (unlike today, when grey-haired hot rodders prefer not to shift gears). I found what I was looking for at Gratiot Auto Supply in nearby Detroit: a 1938 Buick Roadmaster three-speed floorshift transmission for $75 (only half what I paid for the entire car).

Now all I needed was an original 1940 Merc rear end with a torque-tube driveshaft to mate with the back of the Buick transmission, which had been modified to fit into a 1940 Ford that burned rubber and squealed its tires at the Detroit Dragway at Sibley and Dix. I found what I needed by phoning Murray Quick's wrecking yard just outside Leamington. Murray's son Bob delivered a 1940 Merc rear end to me, and the price was good. "Ten bucks, kid," said Bob. It was the only part of my car that never broke down.

The summer was nearly over when I started driving my 1940 Merc around town, mostly with the top down and the hood off. We'd had to remove the floor ahead of the front seat when we installed the transmission — and I never got around to putting it back in. I drove the car off and on for three years and could always see the road passing under my feet.

For the first year, I drove with no exhaust pipes, no mufflers, and no tail pipes (no time, no money). I set fire one day to a girlfriend's parents' front lawn when I parked on the grass and revved up my engine to announce my arrival. Then I looked down through where the floor used to be and saw the grass on fire. The flames from my exhaust manifolds had ignited it. I backed up, jumped out, and stamped out the fire while she stood on her front porch, laughing at me. Then we went for a spin. Luckily for me, her parents weren't home.

As Dad had correctly predicted, the car spent more time in the repair shop than on the road. It kept popping out of third gear, the steering column broke away from the dashboard while I was turning into our driveway, the battery toppled over on another turn, the hood flew off during a road test, the front spring broke off on the QEW, and finally, after three years of aggravation, the clutch linkage broke as I downshifted into second while driving in Toronto, where I now lived.

That was the last straw. I put an ad in the *Toronto Star* and sold it in 1962 to a young man named Marshall Morgan. Two years later he sold it to a young man from Midland, Ontario, and that's when I lost track of it. But I never stopped thinking about it. I kept wondering what had happened to it. Was it scrapped? Was it restored? Was it rebuilt as a street rod? Did it go to the United States? Or, unbeknownst to me, was it stored in someone's garage just around the corner?

In 1988 (twenty-six years after I sold it), I placed an ad in the *Toronto Star* offering a reward of $150 to anyone who could tell me what became of it. I had memorized the serial number when I owned the car, and I included it in the ad.

The only response was from a woman in Milton, Ontario, who told me my car was now owned by a man who worked in a machine shop west of Toronto. I looked at his 1940 Mercury convertible, but it wasn't mine. His had a 1948 Nash dashboard and had been owned by Tony Green in Oakville when I owned mine in Leamington.

In 1990 I ran another ad in the *Toronto Star*. This time Jim Featherstone phoned to tell me that he didn't know where my car was but thought I would like to know that he and Brian Brady bought and sold *fifteen* 1940 Mercury convertibles in Toronto between 1948 and 1950. He showed me lots of photos, and we became good friends, but the search for my long-lost car continued.

When I sold my 1940 Merc to Marshall Morgan in Toronto in 1962, I gave him this photo of the car taken on our front lawn in Leamington in November 1959. He sold the car in 1964 but carried this photo in his wallet for over thirty years. When he learned I had found the car in 1994, he returned the photo to me.

Another three years rolled by with no one coming forward to tell me what had happened to my first car. Finally, a lucky break! My first book on old cars, *The Way We Drove*, was published in October 1993. In November, Dan Proudfoot of the *Toronto Sun* reviewed my book very favourably and mentioned the reward I was offering to anyone who could help me find my first car.

In early December 1993, I attended an antique car parts swap meet at the International Centre in Toronto. There I met Dennis Smith from Stayner, Ontario, who had seen the write-up in the *Toronto Sun* and said he thought he'd bought my car in around 1975. It was a 1940 Mercury convertible parked outside on a turkey farm in Perkinsfield, a small town near Midland, Ontario, where my car had gone in 1964.

"Do you still have the car?" I asked, with my heart in my mouth.

"No," he said, "it was pretty rough so I traded it a year later to Roy Solmes for a 1936 Ford Club Cabriolet in even worse shape."

"Roy Solmes!" I said. "I know Roy. He restores old licence plates."

I phoned Roy that evening at his home in Spring Brook, Ontario. Yes, he remembered owning a 1940 Mercury convertible around 1976 or 1977 — then he sold it to Bill Parm in Belleville.

I got Bill's number from directory assistance and phoned him. He'd owned the 1940 Merc for a year or two, then sold it to his good friend Laverne Allair in nearby Rednersville. He also told me that Laverne still owned it!

I phoned Laverne, and yes, he owned an unrestored 1940 Mercury convertible with a red dashboard and remnants of a white top and white running boards (all pointing to my

Scott Wood of Toronto bought my 1940 Merc in September 2003 when I sold it for the second time. He is doing a magnificent job of rebuilding the car and hopes to have it on the road by the summer of 2005.

car). I asked about the serial number (1D5955). He needed two weeks to find the owner-ship papers, then phoned to tell me that was the serial number of his car!

Sometimes an old car gets scrapped and the ownership paper is used to put an identical make and model back on the road. To make sure that wasn't the case here, I asked Laverne for permission to come and see the car.

On Sunday, January 2, 1994, I headed for Rednersville with Kent Weale, a good friend from my teenage years when I owned the 1940 Merc. Laverne took us to the garage where his car was stored and opened the door.

We looked inside and saw a very weather-beaten old convertible. I could tell by the windshield and vent windows that it was indeed a 1940 Mercury convertible. But was it the one I used to own?

The front fenders were missing, exposing the front suspension to full view. I knelt down for a close look at the passenger side of the transverse front spring, and there in front of me was the proof I was looking for: a square-headed bolt from a hardware store was holding up the end of the spring.

Back in 1961, I was driving my 1940 Merc west on the QEW to visit my old car buddy Peter Clancy in Port Credit, just west of Toronto. Suddenly the front spring on the passenger side broke away from the axle and came down onto the highway. I managed to bring the car to a halt on the gravel shoulder. A tow truck brought me and my car to Peter's house, where we reattached the front spring to the axle using a square-headed bolt from a hardware store.

That same bolt was still holding up the front spring thirty-three years later when Kent and I finally found my long-lost car in Laverne Allair's garage. We also found a dozen other details confirming that the car was the one I had owned so long ago.

Laverne was keeping the car as a retirement project and was not interested in selling it. We took lots of photos, then headed home, happy that we had finally found my first car.

Seven years later, Laverne passed away, and his son offered to sell me the car. I bought it and brought it home to Leamington in April 2001. For the next two years I stored it at Brother Keith Quick's home north of town while I pondered what to do with it. The car had deteriorated badly and needed a great deal of work. I finally decided it was too much for me to tackle, and I sold the car for the second time. Scott Wood bought it in September 2003 and is rebuilding it at his home in Toronto. He is bringing it back to life as a mild mid-fifties custom, exactly what I would have done if I had rebuilt it.

It might be back on the road by the time you read this. I'm looking forward to going for a ride.

CHAPTER TWO:

THREE GENERATIONS OF FIRST CARS By Dave Wolfe

My first car was a 1951 Morris Minor. Dad and I bought it in November 1959 for the grand sum of $40 from the junkyard behind Green Gables Garage in Orillia on my seventeenth birthday. After towing it home behind our 1955 Chevy, we worked on it all winter, doing brakes, freeing up the rusty front suspension, and installing a belt-driven water pump from an old Easy washing machine to pump a bit of warm antifreeze to the Lucas heater core. Never did solve the defroster system, just kept a scraper hanging from the mirror for those frosty winter mornings when I headed off to high school with my pal John and the Chapman girls. Those girls sure knew how to steam up the car windows in a hurry!

When spring came, the little car was sanded and body-filled in our backyard and soon sported a shiny coat of Canadian Tire MotoMaster green, carefully applied with the best roller-coater CTC could supply for two bucks. Next came some light grey deep pile carpet, cut and fitted from our neighbour's old living room rug. The biggest expense was a brand new set of Port-a-Walls from Canadian Tire, and once they were installed there was no turning back. We were on the road to a summer of fun! [Author's note: For those too young to remember, Port-a-Walls were molded rings of white rubber that we used to attach between the bead and the rim flange to make our old blackwalls look like new whitewall tires. They worked well for slow cruising, but at high speed they had a tendency to pull away from the tire with sad results.]

I became a member of the Twin Lakes Motor Club, an active sports car club that met in the showroom of the aforementioned Green Gables Garage, the local MG and Austin Healey dealer, and the little Minor was my ticket to ride with the real car guys. In those days it was common for dealers to bring new models to the local car clubs to introduce them to potential buyers, and in spite of the occasional salesman's protest, the older guys in the club always made sure that I had my turn for a test drive. Daimler Dart SP250, first Mini-Minor in Canada, prototype Mark 2 Sprite, big Healeys, Jaguars, Porsches — I was in car heaven.

The Morris and I ran in club rallies, pit crewed for club racers at Harewood and Green Acres, even toured Mosport Park on a club picnic while the course was still gravel. After the track was paved and open, we went camping to the first Players 200 and slept in the back seat with the sleeping bag poked through into the trunk. The faithful little Morris Minor ran along at 25 miles per gallon of gas and 200 miles per quart of SAE 30 for two of the best summers of my youth and gave me a love for cars that is still going strong today.

My friend Pat came by recently to tell me that he had just seen a Morris Minor with an Orillia dealer's tag for sale at Ron Fawcett's in Whitby. Did I want to go for a look? My heart said, "Yes!!" but better judgment prevailed. I'm sorry. It would not be roller-coated in MotoMaster green, and I can never be seventeen again.

Dave Wolfe's first car: fresh from the junkyard.

One weekend in about 1975, my friends Roy and Barb and I were heading to a Ford Reunion car show. Our little T-Birds were tuned up and polished, and Roy's was sporting a brand new set of Port-a-Walls. Heading across 401 on our way to Oakville, Roy decided to give his Bird a run "to clean out the carbon." As he blew past me at a rather illegal velocity, the wind caught the edge of the Port-a-Walls, violently ripping them off of the tires, leaving only a few torn frills of white rubber where the fake whitewalls had been just seconds before. When we left the registration desk in front of the Ford Plant, the 1955 Bird with the frilly rims did another trick common to old six-volt systems on hot engines. It suffered a heatstroke and refused to start in front of the crowd. Luckily it had a standard transmission, and a quick bump start in second gear got her moving. We put our cars in the display area and went around taking photographs of the finer Fords on display. When the frame counter in his new camera passed twenty-four, Roy decided he must have put in a thirty-six-shot film. When the counter passed thirty-seven later in the afternoon, a little cloud began to form over his head, and when he opened the camera to find there was no film inside, it was pretty much time to go home!

I have been around car buffs for a long time, and there are always stories of "the day we blew the motor at Mosport" and "the day we blew the tranny in the Duster," but that trip to the Ford plant will always be remembered as "the day we blew the Port-a-Walls off the Bird."

My dad, Jerry Wolfe's, first car started off its life as a 1919 Ford Model T two-passenger coupe with styling that could most charitably be described as a telephone booth on wheels. Dad bought it in 1925, and it was well used by then, on the rough roads in and around the city of Winnipeg where Dad was raised. In the cold of a Manitoba winter, the heaterless old Model T was a pretty cool car temperature-wise, and young Jerry, the engineering student, devised a plan to warm things up for the passengers. He stretched a large sheet of canvas from the bottom of the radiator back under the engine and clamped it to the edges of the running boards on each side.

In theory, this would trap all of the engine heat and force some of it up through a neatly cut hole in the wooden floorboards, thereby warming up driver and companion. In practice, however, the results were much more spectacular. The canvas got nicely oil-soaked by the leaky old four-banger, and on a winter run out to Headingly, the wind blew the oily rag onto the hot exhaust, igniting it, sending flames through the hole in the floor and into the cab. Not much choice but to aim her at the nearest snowbank and bail out, hoping that the snow would douse the flames.

After the remains were hauled back home, the question became, "What can a young guy do with the charred hulk of a 1919 Model T coupe?" The answer, of course, was obvious to Jerry and his mates. "We'll make a bug roadster out of it." So, in the summer of 1926, the car in the picture was born. The telephone booth body went to the scrap dealer. The cowl and engine compartment were cleaned up and rewired, and a sporty wooden windshield complete with wiper was constructed on a homebuilt sheet metal body. To finish off the rear of this 1926 hot rod he needed a trunk, so he used a real one. The steamer trunk that his father had used to emigrate from England was dragged up from the cellar and mounted proudly on the back of the little bug roadster. A folding top was scavenged from an old runabout, and the bug was ready to go.

Jerry was a radio enthusiast in its pioneering days and earned his tuition and spending money doing in-home radio service calls for the Hudson's Bay Company. The bug roadster could be seen most evenings and Saturdays carrying Jerry and his tool kit along the avenues in the ritzy parts of the 'Peg looking for a stately home with a wonky radio. I am sure the maid would have asked him to park it around back!

On summer Sundays and holidays it was a ride to the Canoe Club for tennis or north to Boundary Park for a sail on Lake Winnipeg. In winter, Winnipeg was not a great place for a roadster. There was speed skating and cross-country skiing, but getting there was not half the fun. First, you had to warm up the engine cooling water (which you had drained the night before if you were expecting cold weather) by heating it on the wood stove. After pouring the hot coolant into the radiator, if the thermometer was near twenty or thirty below, it usually took a buddy outside on the crank and Jerry inside on throttle, spark lever, and electric starter to get the engine motivated. Then, with teeth chattering from the cold and bones shaking from heavy rope wound around the skinny tires to add some grip in the snow, they were under the old buffalo robes and off on a winter adventure.

My grandfather, Norval Davison, was a bit older than most of us when he got his first car. At the age of thirty-four, he was operating a successful bicycle shop, but he had the foresight to realize that the new automobiles would be the wave of the future. According to family history, Norval owned the first car in Winnipeg. He certainly owned the first Cadillac in Winnipeg. The 1903 Cadillac Model A in this old family photo was one of three purchased from the Cadillac Automobile Company of Detroit and shipped to Manitoba in knocked-down form by train. The cars were assembled in the Davison bicycle shop and offered for sale. The Davison family spent summer holidays with their cousins, the Rutherfords, in the little town of Stonewall, north of Winnipeg, and the new Cadillac motorcar created quite a stir when it came to town. It was the first car most of the local people had ever seen.

Painted and ready to roll.

Jerry's bug roadster.

The Davison family 1903 Cadillac.

Grandfather learned to drive and to sell cars, and soon the bicycle shop turned into an auto shop, which grew to become one of the earliest Winnipeg garages. By trade, Norval Davison was what we now call a body man. He originally apprenticed as a carriage painter and master pinstriper as a young man in 1885, and many of the cars he sold received special decorative striping jobs to personalize them to the customer's taste. In those days, you could buy a new two-seater Cadillac for $750. The rear door tonneau added two back seats for only $100 more (a bit of a jump to the $79,215 list price for a 2004 Escalade ESV!).

In 1919, Norval moved to Hollywood, California, to open a new dealership with his brother Charles, but in the period after the end of the First World War, there was a lot of turmoil in the automotive industry, and in the late 1920s the California business failed. The Davisons returned to the Chicago area, where Norval became the agent for the Pantasote Company, selling a newly developed product for automotive and railway upholstery, the embossed vinyl-covered canvas we all know as Leatherette or Naugahyde.

The little boy getting his first ride in the back seat of the 1903 Cadillac is my uncle, Bryden Davison. After a long career with General Motors in Detroit, Bryden retired to Arizona and bought himself a new 1966 Cadillac Sedan de Ville. He had his first car ride in a Cadillac, and he ended his driving career in one. The 1966 Caddy stayed in our family, and I still keep her polished up and ready for special occasions and summer cruising.

CHAPTER THREE:

DOUG LENNOX REMEMBERS A 1949 CHEVY

It was a 1949 Chevrolet four-door sedan, grey in colour and purchased for $300 in around 1956 in Sudbury, Ontario, by Doug Lennox (then eighteen) and his friend Dave Weir. Both fellows were still living at home with their parents and knew their folks would not be happy with this purchase.

They got around this by keeping the car first at one house, then the other, and saying, "It's not my car. It belongs to my friend, and he has to park it here because his parents don't want him to have a car." This line worked well at both houses, and the parents apparently never caught on.

Lucky for them they never did. Doug and Dave's 1949 Chevy was an accident looking for a place to happen. Every time they stepped on the brakes, fluid squirted out of the master cylinder. This was particularly nerve-wracking every time they drove down a hill toward a T-intersection. They couldn't afford to have the master cylinder repaired or replaced (all their spare cash went into the gas tank), so they carried a big can of brake fluid in the car and topped up the master cylinder whenever the brake pedal sank dangerously close to the floor.

And down on the floor was another problem. The gas pedal kept sticking to the floor, running the risk of the car accelerating out of control and/or blowing the engine. Doug and Dave solved this problem with youthful ingenuity by attaching a string to the top of the gas pedal and the other end to the driver. If the pedal stuck to the floor, they gave the string a yank.

The original cloth interior was looking pretty ratty, so the boys cut some cloth and made some slipcovers. This made the interior more inviting whenever the boys took girls out on dates. They often drove to the local drive-in to catch a movie, then parked in the moonlight beside one of the many nearby lakes. There were lots of places for parking and necking — so many, in fact, that Doug remembers Sudbury as "the make-out capital of North America."

Doug kept some condoms in the glove compartment (just in case), but he never got to use them because his mother found them first. You'll remember Doug claimed the car belonged to Dave. "Gosh, Mom, those must be Dave's. After all, it's his car."

Doug and Dave owned their 1949 Chevy just as the rock 'n' roll explosion was turning the world of music upside down. The car had a radio — but if the boys and their friends didn't care for the song coming out of the dashboard, they turned the radio down and sang all their favourite songs in harmony.

The most Beautiful BUY of all!

"I'm biding my time until I get a Chevrolet—

I want to be sure I get the most for my money!"

● That expresses the sentiments of countless people in all income groups, including many who can afford to buy much higher-priced cars. They're surveying the rest but awaiting the best — Chevrolet—*the most beautiful buy of all!* We believe you, too, will decide that Chevrolet gives more for your money — more fine-car beauty, more fine-car features, more EXTRA VALUES of all kinds — at the *lowest* prices and with outstanding economy of operation and upkeep. Yes, the new Chevrolet is the most beautiful buy for everything from styling to stamina, and we cordially invite you to confirm this fact and tell your friends — *"I'm biding my time until I get a Chevrolet!"*

Insist on getting these EXTRA VALUES exclusive to Chevrolet in its field!

● World's Champion Valve-In-Head Engine
● Fisher Body Styling and Luxury
● Fisher Unisteel Body Construction
● Certi-Safe Hydraulic Brakes (with Dubl-Life Rivetless Brake Linings)
● Longest, Heaviest Car in Its Field *with Widest* Tread, *as well*
● 5-inch Wide-Base Wheels (with Extra-Low-Pressure Tires)
● Centre-Point Steering
● Curved Windshield *with Panoramic Visibility*
● Extra-Economical to Own – Operate – Maintain

A PRODUCT OF GENERAL MOTORS

Styleline De Luxe 4-Door Sedan

WIGLE MOTORS LIMITED

Chevrolet and Oldsmobile Cars — Chevrolet Trucks

Telephone 169   LEAMINGTON   58 Erie St. North

Leamington Post & News, *April 21, 1949.*

The good times couldn't last forever, and after a year or so on the road, Doug and Dave sold their first car to Greenspoon Brothers junkyard for scrap. They got $65 for it. The car should have gone to the junkyard before the boys bought it. So many things were wrong with it, Doug looks back today and says, "We're lucky to be alive."

Other cars soon came into Doug's life, including a white 1956 Ford Fairlane convertible ("I'd love to have it now"). Many other convertibles followed, including the 1971 MGB sports car he acquired in 1972.

He was prompted to hang onto it when production of North American convertibles ended in 1976. When convertible production resumed around 1983, Doug was so attached to his MGB that he couldn't let it go. It's dark blue, restored, and beautiful. He still owns it and drives it every summer.

Doug Lennox is well known through his thirty-five years as a freelance writer, producer, and host in Canadian radio and television. His work at the CBC with such legends as Anne Murray, Sylvia Tyson, Oscar Peterson, Anton Kuerti, and Ronnie Hawkins, among a host of others, has won him acclaim and international recognition. As an actor, he has been featured in many movies and television dramas, including *X-Men*, *The Herd*, *Nero Wolfe*, *Odyssey 5*, and *Against the Ropes*.

Doug is also well-known today to the one million listeners of his nationally syndicated radio show, *Now You Know*, heard daily on CFRB and now the title of his recent Canadian bestseller, followed by *Now You Know More* (both published by Dundurn Press in Toronto, the same people who brought you the book you are now reading).

Doug Lennox has come a long way from the day nearly fifty years ago when he purchased one-half of a 1949 Chevrolet.

CHAPTER FOUR:

BOB JAMES REMEMBERS HIS 1957 FORD CONVERTIBLE

It wasn't his first car. It wasn't even his first convertible. But it was the first convertible he owned with tail fins. He drove it over forty years ago, and he still remembers that car as if he bought it yesterday.

Now in his early seventies, Bob James was born on January 28, 1934, and grew up in the French-Canadian town of Sayabec, Quebec. He bought his first car in Montreal in 1952 when he was eighteen. It was a 1938 Plymouth two-door sedan. He and his pals drove it around town every Saturday night till they ran out of money and out of gas. Then they pushed it home. (See page 118.)

His next car was much flashier — a chrome-clobbered two-tone 1941 Ford convertible. (See page 51.) He bolted the spare tire to the outside of the trunk lid, repainted the entire car "Banff Blue," then stepped on the gas till he smashed into the back of a truck.

He removed all the mangled and twisted metal, then drove the car to work every day for the next two weeks with the entire front part of the car missing. The police never pulled him over. Just try that today.

In March 1954 Bob traded in his 1941 ragtop at Hart Motors for an incredibly rare 1947 Ford Sportsman wood-bodied convertible, possibly the only one in Canada at that time. He drove that car for two years, then sold it, still running, for $200. The full story

Bob James stands with pride alongside his repaired and repainted 1957 Ford Fairlane 500 convertible in Sept-Iles, Quebec, in 1960. The car is parked in front of Quebec-Newfoundland Equipment and Supply. Bob owned this flashy fliptop for nearly two years, then traded it for a 1959 Ford station wagon in Montreal in November 1961. The car is gone, but the memories are still as fresh as yesterday. Says Bob, "I wish I had it now."

Not yet ready for the junkyard. Bob James purchased this smashed-up 1957 Ford convertible for $500. It was only two years old.

On the road to recovery. Bob now has new front end sheet metal on his 1957 Ford and is getting it ready for a repaint job. Note the hood hinges. From 1957 to 1959, Ford hoods were hinged at the front and opened from the back.

of Bob's 1947 Ford is in my previous book, *60 Years Behind the Wheel*.

Other cars came and went as Bob drove his way through the late 1950s. When he told me recently that he had owned a 1957 Ford Fairlane 500 convertible in Quebec in 1960, I asked him to tell me all about it. We met in the living room of Bob's nephew's home in Toronto. I turned on my little tape recorder, and Bob was off to the races:

"Here's the way this story starts on my 1957 Ford convertible. I worked on the St. Lawrence Seaway, and I had a company car. Then the Seaway was finished by the fall of 1959 and they didn't know where to put me, 'they' being Goodyear Tire. A lot of the heavy equipment used on the Seaway now had to go to a new deep-sea dock being opened up at Port-Cartier near Sept-Iles, or Seven Islands, and a lot of the Euclid earth movers and other heavy equipment went up there. They needed a man up there to look after these big tires, like I had done on the Seaway, so it was natural for me to go.

"They put me in touch with Quebec-Newfoundland Equipment and Supply, which was all part of Clark Steamships. They had the wholesale Esso business in Seven Islands, they owned the big grocery store there, and they were the local Goodyear Tire wholesaler. They even had a retread shop. So I agreed to go, and it was good money. The only way to get there then was to fly in. There's a road to there now, but there wasn't back then.

"I arrived there in the fall of 1959, and they gave me a company car because they also had the local Mercury-Meteor dealership. They sent for a brand new Mercury truck, which took a few months, and it arrived with the Goodyear colours. So now I've got a brand new truck and I'm getting to know people there. I was living with the local OPP man and his wife and two children, and I rented a room there.

"So we're working away, and I guess it was the spring of 1960, I get to the shop one day and there's a smashed-up 1957 Ford convertible in the yard, with a continental kit. I like cars and I thought it was a shame, so I inquired, and it would be for sale 'as is' for $500. So I bought it."

I asked, "Did they tell you what caused the accident?"

Bob answered, "No, they didn't. So the first thing, of course, we have to get it fixed. I was making good money there, and I found a fellow who worked in our shop. He was a body man and he came from Rimouski and he had contacts in Rimouski. So, to make a long story short, we found a bumper and a used grille and a used right front fender. Then I hired a fellow to take the whole front end off and we put the new stuff on.

"And I learned a very valuable lesson. I had given him — I don't think I paid him *all* in advance, it could be two or three hundred dollars — but he didn't have the ambition to work on it because he had spent the money. So I got after him, and finally, as you can see in the pictures, the right fender was fixed up pretty good …"

"And the car originally was black?"

What a beauty! As soon as Bob's convertible came out of the paint shop, he parked it where he first saw it and took this photo.

"It was black with red and white inside, but I knew at the time not to paint a fixed-up car black. If there was a wave, it would show, and I never liked black. Black is for funeral cars. The only other option was white. I forget just who did the paint — I guess the guy there — and of course, as you see in the pictures, I took a picture as I found it and then I drove it right back to the same spot and took a picture when it was all fixed up, it's sort of before and after. Same shed and everything. Actually, the shed in behind is the retread shop. And the St. Lawrence River is right behind it. The company was Quebec-Newfoundland Equipment and Supply.

"Now here's a funny story. I had the car, but I still had the company truck. I parked the car out in front of where I stayed with the OPP across the street. I got up one morning to look out at my beautiful car and the left front hubcap was missing. This was a wheel disc. I didn't drive it all that much and I wasn't rough with the car. I went out and looked at the other side and the other disc was gone too. So I knew then they were stolen.

"At the same time up at the new garage was a 1957 500 sedan with the engine out of it, like a used car, so being a very honest fellow I went into the back seat and got my two wheel discs, and an hour later they were on my car. And so whoever stole them would probably see me driving around — and he must have wondered how fast I got them."

Here's young Bob James (only twenty-seven) with the 1959 Ford station wagon he purchased from the Cumming-Perrault dealership in Montreal in November 1961. His trade-in was his 1957 Ford Fairlane 500 convertible.

"I notice you had fender skirts on the car. Do you think the skirts saved the rear discs from being stolen?"

"I don't know if they were on at that time. I probably bought them when I got back to Montreal. Anyway, the car was there in Seven Islands, and I used it and had the top down, and it was one of the nicest cars there. I finished up there in the fall of 1960. My boss left for his annual vacation in a nice 1959 hardtop and I left the next day. I had my money and I left.

"I got back to Montreal and I got a job with B.F. Goodrich. I still had the 1957 convertible, and it was my everyday car. Now in those years, if your car had a clock in the dash, it would go fast or slow …"

I commented, "Those clocks were notorious for not telling the right time."

Bob responded, "Maybe it was because of the accident, but I never used my watch again. The clock in my car never lost a second. It was the best clock I ever had. The shock of the accident might have given it the right adjustment.

"Now, I kept the convertible for only a year or so, it was getting old, and around 1961 I found at Cumming-Perrault a 1959 Ford station wagon, grey with red and white inside. I decided to make a trade. Now at this point I'm going out with jobber salesmen to promote our products at B.F. Goodrich, and we went all over the place. So I made arrangements to buy the station wagon and I would pick it up the following Saturday …"

"And this was at the Cumming-Perrault Ford dealership. Where were they located, Bob?"

"On Upper Lachine Road in Montreal. So I'm coming in from being out in Three Rivers or somewhere, and there's a big hole that never seemed to get fixed on Cote de Liesse Road (I lived out in Pointe Claire). I'm coming home in the convertible and I'm tired and I'm looking forward to getting my new vehicle the next day and I hit this hole — *thump!* — right in the middle. One heck of a bang. But anyway, I made it home.

"The next morning, of course, I hopped into the car and I'm going in to Cumming-Perrault and I parked it there. I saw the salesman, he gave me my new keys, I gave him my keys to the convertible. He told me I'd have to come back next week to have something fixed, so I said okay. This is now about November 1961."

"And your new station wagon — was it an automatic or stick shift?"

"Automatic. Even in those days I didn't like a stick shift. So, next week, sometime during the week I go back to Cumming-Perrault and I go to see the guy. 'Oh, are you ever lucky!' he says. And I say, 'What do you mean?' And he says, 'Well, the yard fellow went to move the convertible and a front wheel fell off.' I must have cracked the front suspension when I hit that pothole. They had to get a tow truck. The wheel actually fell off. Imagine if it had done that while I was driving I would have had to fix all that."

"And besides, you might have been killed."

"It was that big hole that finished it off. I enjoyed the convertible while I had it. It was still in pretty good shape. I forget the mileage on it. That might show up on all the receipts I saved. And I'll tell you this: I wish I had that car now. It had the proper continental kit on it and everything …"

CHAPTER FIVE

KENT WEALE REMEMBERS HIS 1940 FORD COUPE

In April 1960, Kent Weale of Port Credit, Ontario, bought his first car, a 1940 Ford Deluxe coupe. He had turned sixteen just three months earlier — on January 16, 1960 — and was itching to put himself on the road. He got his sixty-day learner's permit the day after his birthday. And two days after that, he broke his ankle while skiing, spent a week in the hospital, and hobbled around for the next two months with his ankle in a cast. The physical pain was nothing compared to the agony suffered by the young Mr. Weale as he waited for the day when he could slide behind the wheel.

By April, Kent was as good as new. He got his permanent driver's licence and then — unbeknownst to his parents — went out and bought himself a car! He saw two ads in the paper. One was for a Model A Ford roadster pickup with an Olds engine, but this vehicle was nowhere near ready for the road. The other was for a 1940 Ford Deluxe coupe in the west end of Toronto. Kent's half-brother accompanied him that day and assured him that the 1940 coupe was "more of a car" than the Model A. That's all the prodding that Kent needed. He forked over exactly $200 (no sales tax back then) from his part-time earnings and the car was his. It was twenty years old, but it still ran. It wouldn't start when the engine was hot — but who cared? Just open the hood for a few minutes to cool it down and away we go!

The front seat was covered in green and white slipcovers from Canadian Tire, but the two opera seats in the back were still covered in the original mohair (or something that looked like mohair). There was no radio, just the factory-installed cover plate on the dash, but the car did have a cowl-mounted aerial. That meant whenever Kent went for a drive, everyone would think he had a radio.

Unlike my 1940 Merc ragtop (see page 11), which had to be pushed all the way home the day I bought it, Kent had the luxury of driving his newly acquired 1940 Ford all the way home under its own power. (Kent's half-brother followed close behind in his late 1950s Mercury, just in case.) A 1948 Merc flathead was under Kent's hood, and included in the deal was a not-yet-installed dual carb intake manifold.

Kent pulled into the driveway at home, thinking his mom and dad were out for the day. But it was impossible to conceal his new acquisition for long. It was truly an automobile of incomparable distinction with its grey body, pink fenders and roof, and black trunk lid. A car screaming to be noticed.

Kent's dad hated Fords. At this time, he was driving a one-year-old Cadillac — a 1959. It was a very conservative black four-door sedan purchased new from Addison Cadillac at 832 Bay Street (where they still are today). In fact, Kent's dad had driven Cadillacs for as long as Kent could remember (except for one black Packard back in the 1940s).

Dad was very upset when he saw his son's multi-coloured 1940 Ford in the driveway — then calmed down enough to get his camera and take a picture of the car with Kent behind the wheel. Then he ordered Kent to put it in the garage (probably so the neighbours wouldn't have to look at it).

The next day he called a tow truck and had the car towed away — not to a wrecking yard but to Webster Jackman Motors,

First day home with the 1940 Ford coupe at 1566 Pinetree Crescent in Port Credit (now Mississauga). Was Kent's dad ever mad! But he cooled down enough to take this photo later that day. Body colours are pink (roof and fenders), black (trunk lid), and grey (everything else). Note block of wood behind the rear wheel. Also note large dent in driver's door. Kent definitely bought this car "as is."

a Mercury-Meteor dealership in Streetsville owned and operated by Kent's dad's best friend. Dad insisted the brakes and steering be checked over and the bald tires be replaced with a new set.

He refused to pay extra for whitewalls, so Kent rushed to the nearest Canadian Tire store for a can of whitewall tire paint. He painted wider whitewalls on the rear tires to make them look bigger than the front ones, and he used the leftover paint to make his running boards white. This car was well on its way to becoming super-cool.

Kent's father did not share his son's enthusiasm for cool cars and squelched Kent's plans for rerouting the gas filler neck to inside the trunk. Kent's 1940 Ford came with two new rear fenders, and the hole for the gas filler neck on the left rear had already been filled in. But Kent's dad would not tolerate the risk of gas fumes in the trunk, so Kent reluctantly punched out the filled-in hole before installing the new rear fenders.

But from that point on, this was Kent Weale's car all the way. He installed a two-and-a-half-inch dropped front axle to give the car a California rake. He also installed the dual carb intake manifold that came with the car and rounded up another Stromberg 97. A special arm had to be purchased from a hot rod shop to relocate the generator out of the way of the front carburetor.

To keep the horsepower climbing, Kent replaced the stock exhaust manifolds on the 1948 Merc flathead with headers, then added dual exhausts with Canadian Tire glass-pak mufflers, flexible exhaust pipes, and stock tailpipes. The huge chrome tailpipe extensions he added kept falling off, so Kent drilled a hole and put a big bolt right through each extension and tailpipe. Now his car not only went much faster, it looked much faster too!

By this time, the multi-coloured exterior was history. Soon after buying the car, Kent wheeled it into the family garage and sprayed the body with thirteen hand-held cans of blue paint from Canadian Tire. The result looked so awful that Kent's dad opened his wallet again and treated the car to a professional paint job. Same colour, but what a difference!

Kent carried the blue colour scheme into the engine compartment when he installed the dual carb manifold. The gas was delivered to the carburetors in blue neoprene hoses to harmonize with the gleaming blue exterior finish. Details like this put Kent's car a cut above your average hot-rodded 1940 Ford coupe. As a final touch to the exterior, Kent installed spun aluminum wheel discs and then drove around town looking at his reflection in store windows. To throw faster shifts, Kent replaced the stock "three on the tree" column shift with a 1939 Ford floorshift gearbox from an auto wreckers. This meant cutting a hole in the floor. Kent's dad had a fit when he saw the hole, but the floorshift stayed.

Kent now power-shifted every time he drove the car, but the stock gears were not designed for that kind of punishment. He stripped one gear after another (if his father only knew!) and ultimately went through eight sets of gears. The only gear he never stripped was reverse. The first time he took out the transmission, it took him two days of back-breaking, knuckle-bruising labour. After lots of practice, he got it down to two hours.

The final straw came when the transmission failed out in Scarborough and Kent had to be towed all the way home behind his cousin's 1954 Chevy sedan. At this point, Kent decided to switch to Lincoln gears. He bought a set from a local car enthusiast, and they dropped right into the 1939 Ford gearbox. The Lincoln gears were much stronger, and now Kent really poured on the gas.

Kent's father was in the hotel building business and got the contract to install all the electrical circuitry in the O'Keefe Centre when it was under construction. And he was invited to attend the grand opening in the fall of 1960.

He and Mrs. Weale couldn't make it that night, so Kent ended up with their two tickets. He and his girlfriend climbed into the 1940 Ford and rumbled right up to the front entrance amid Cadillacs and Lincolns disgorging men in tuxedos and ladies in evening gowns. Luckily, the door handle didn't fall off when the uniformed doorman opened the passenger door to let Kent's date out. Then Kent crept forward to find a parking spot.

In the spring of 1962, after serving Kent faithfully for two years, the 1948 Merc flathead under the hood no longer satisfied Kent's craving for more horsepower. The time had come to drop an overhead-valve engine into the 1940 Ford. Kent loved the look of the horizontal rocker covers on the Buick V8 (first introduced in 1953) and snapped one up from a local wrecking yard for about $100. Kent had it delivered to the house while his parents were down south on vacation.

The engine swap had to be done fast (in other words, before Mom and Dad got home). Kent borrowed a block and tackle from our mutual friend Peter Clancy, who also helped Kent with the actual installation. Kent hung the block and tackle from the overhead beam inside his parents' garage and braced the beam with extra supports so that the weight of the Buick engine would not bring the garage roof crashing down on top of them.

To reduce the cost of the engine swap for Kent, Peter lined up someone with an old Ford pickup truck that needed a replacement engine. This truck was driven to the house and was parked in Kent's double-car garage right beside his car. As soon as they yanked the 1948 Merc flathead out of the car, they dropped it into the old truck and hooked it up. The owner of the truck then drove off, bringing Kent to the point of no return. Now he *had* to drop the Buick engine in — it was the only engine he had.

Kent and Pete hoisted the Buick engine into the air and rolled the 1940 Ford underneath it. As they lowered it into the engine compartment, they discovered it wouldn't fit because the distributor hit the firewall and cracked the distributor cap before they could bolt the Buick engine to the Ford transmission.

This came as a great surprise because Kent and Pete had a mutual friend named George Phemister who had recently purchased a 1940 Ford Tudor with no engine in it. George had been told by the previous owner that a Buick engine could be dropped right into the 1940 Tudor with no problem. What Kent and Pete did not realize at the time was that the firewall on the 1940 Tudor had been carefully notched to allow clearance for the

Buick distributor. (That previous owner, by the way, was Marshall Morgan, the young man who bought my 1940 Merc convertible later that year.)

Because they were racing against the clock on this engine swap, Kent and Pete hoisted the Buick engine up out of the way, then climbed into the engine compartment and attacked the firewall with a hammer and chisel. A huge chunk of the firewall fell off, taking with it the linkage connecting the gas pedal to the carburetor.

Now the engine cleared the firewall with lots of room to spare, but as they lowered the engine into place, the starter motor hit the steering box, making it impossible to connect the engine to the front motor mounts. Kent, with mounting panic, looked at Pete, who already had the answer: "No problem. We'll take off the starter motor and worry about that later."

Off it came, and in went the new engine. Canadian Tire supplied the flexible exhaust pipes from the engine to the muffler. A twelve-volt battery was needed for the engine, so that went in too, and Pete tapped a bolt into the middle of the battery to supply six-volt current to the rest of the car.

To make room for the starter motor, Kent and Pete disconnected the steering box, then reattached it one inch forward and one inch down from its original position. The steering column bracket below the firewall had to be loosened, and now the steering wheel was a little closer to the dashboard.

The car could now be started, but it wouldn't go into gear. Kent asked a mechanic at a local gas station what the problem might be. After the mechanic stopped laughing, he told Kent the clutch disc was in backwards. Because Kent had changed the transmission so many times before, he knew exactly what to do: jack up the rear end, roll it back with its torque-tube driveshaft, then yank out the transmission, unbolt the pressure plate, turn the clutch disc around, and put everything back together. All this

Kent enjoyed a summer romance with Cynthia Robinson — his first summer with the 1940 Ford coupe. They met in the Port Severn, Ontario, area near the Weales' family cottage.

work took an extra half-day and proved the truth of Gumperson's Law: If you have a 50 percent chance of getting something right, you'll get it wrong.

Now the car was ready for the road, with a coat hanger through the dashboard and fire-wall to the carburetor to replace the accelerator linkage chiselled off the previous day. To shift gears, Kent had to take both hands off the wheel and steer the car with his left elbow and right knee.

The swap was completed before Kent's parents returned home, but the next-door neighbour blabbed all about it to them two days later.

"My dad was ready to kill me," says Kent over forty years later. "He insisted I fix the accelerator, so I remounted and rerouted the linkage."

A new problem cropped up now that the car was on the road. The Buick engine kept overheating because the fan blades had to be shortened

Kent poses with pride in the family driveway with his new paint job, whitewall tires, moon discs, and white running boards.

three inches to clear the upper rad hose going into the 1940 Ford rad. This problem was never solved. However, Kent learned to live with it. He could drive the car around town for about ten minutes before it started boiling over, then he headed for the open highway to cool it down.

Shortly before the engine swap, Kent pulled up to a red light on Lakeshore Road in Port Credit, less than a mile from home. A guy pulled up alongside in a maroon 1940 Ford coupe and challenged Kent to a drag. The light turned green, and Kent shoved his foot to the floor. The dual carbs and dual exhaust put Kent out in front, and he beat the other 1940 Ford easily.

Two weeks after the engine swap, Kent pulled up to that same red light on Lakeshore Road. And by sheer coincidence, the same maroon 1940 Ford coupe pulled up beside him to a drag once again. The driver in the maroon Ford was feeling supremely confident because he had installed an Olds engine in his car a few days earlier and thought Kent was still running his flathead. Then the light turned green and Kent beat him again!

The 1940 Ford took Kent many places, including several round trips to the family cottage on the Severn River. But sooner or later, most people sell their car, and this car was no exception. Around the end of the summer of 1962, Kent sold the car to our mutual friend Peter Clancy, who promptly sold it to Bill Yundt, a Port Credit hot rodder who had sold me a 1940 Merc convertible parts car a year earlier.

Yundt also sold the 1940 coupe, and it changed hands two or three times over the next couple of years. Kent heard through the grapevine that someone had dropped an Olds engine into it, and then it was purchased by Ron Cole, who installed a Cadillac engine. When Cole road-tested the car to see what it could do, he quickly found out. The Cadillac engine cranked out so much horsepower, it ripped the rear end right out of the car. Kent doesn't know what became of his Ford after that, except to say it might be in Orangeville, Ontario.

He drove his mom's 1956 Chevy for a while, then bought another old car the following year — a purple 1951 Monarch convertible. And that's another story!

CHAPTER SIX:

JOHN SQUIRREL'S FIRST (AND LAST) 1939 MERCURY CONVERTIBLE

By John Squirrel

On January 7, 2003, John Squirrel of Okanagan Falls, British Columbia,
wrote the following letter to the Old Car Detective.

Dear Bill Sherk,

Way back in 1952 I was employed by a company in Toronto named Garage Supply as an automotive machinist apprentice. Rebored engines, did heads, fitted pins, etc.

A good friend and I became stock car enthusiasts and spent lots of time going to Exhibition and Pinecrest and other tracks around Toronto. At that time I had a 1941 Ford Deluxe business coupe. We got a chance to drive a stock one evening at the Exhibition grounds — not a race, just once around the track, and that hooked us into thinking we should build a car. The deal my friend and I made was he would supply the vehicle and I would build the engine. I found a good 59A block and started in and eventually built as potent a flathead engine as any around. In the meantime, my friend suddenly got married, and that shot down his participation and left me with a great engine and no place to shove it in. I'd sold my 1941 Ford and was riding a famous James 125cc bike.

In those days Danforth Avenue was used car alley, and the further east you went, the lower the quality of the cars got. East of Victoria Park were a series of these lots, and on the worst of the worst I found a 1939 Merc convertible.

The windshield header for the top was made of wood and was almost totally rotted away, and the engine smoked so bad there were no mosquitoes left in Scarborough. The body was not rusted, but it had its fair share of dings and dangs. The price of $25 (knocked down from $40) was about all I could afford, and the deal was made. I very facetiously asked if there was any warranty, and the salesman said, "I guarantee it will get off the lot." It didn't make it. Front wheels over the curb and it died. True to his word, the lot man installed a new fuel pump, about $1.25 in those days. I limped this thing about three blocks to a rented garage near Victoria Park and Danforth.

Took a while for me to do the engine swap, as I'd never done one before, but a couple of weeks later the thing got started and I took my first real ride. Did this thing ever go!

Thirty-five years ago, the Ford Motor Company manufactured its first automobile. The accumulated experience of all those thirty-five years now finds new expression in an entirely new car, the Mercury 8 . . . designed to extend Ford-Lincoln standards of mechanical excellence, progressive design and outstanding value to a new price field.

THE NEW

MERCURY 8

A PRODUCT OF THE FORD MOTOR COMPANY

There's something as new as the Spring in the clean, sweeping lines of the Mercury 8. It is a wide, remarkably roomy car, but skilful design has made its bulk beautiful. • There's extra smoothness and silence, too, as well as extra space. Soundproofing materials help to eliminate noise and vibration. Restful quiet is as much a part of Mercury comfort as are soft, deep seats. • The Mercury has hydraulic brakes and a brilliant, economical new 95-horsepower V-type 8-cylinder engine. All its appointments are as modern as the new steering wheel and instrument panel shown at right.

FORD MOTOR COMPANY . . . FORD, MERCURY, LINCOLN-ZEPHYR AND LINCOLN MOTOR CARS

FEATURES OF THE MERCURY 8

116-inch wheelbase; 16 feet, 4 inches over-all length • Unusual width and room for passengers • 95-horsepower V-type 8-cylinder engine • Hydraulic brakes • Modern flowing lines • Luxurious appointments and upholstery • Deep, soft seat construction • Thorough scientific soundproofing • Balanced weight distribution and center-poise design • Large luggage compartments.

Ford-Built Means Top Value

This ad featuring the new 1939 Mercury convertible appeared in National Geographic magazine in May 1939.

Sadly, the brakes were not up to the engine (they weren't up to the old one either). So another week went by as I rebuilt master and wheel cylinders, turned drums and relined all wheels. Yahoo, now I can go and stop.

What's this violent shimmy at about 50 miles per hour? King pins and tie rods — what the heck are they? There is much to be said for safety checks on vehicles before they are sold. Once again into my Mickey Mouse garage.

I learned real fast how a Hot Wrench works to help get apart frozen front end parts. Thank the Lord for where I worked, as I could borrow most of the tools I needed, except I was so clueless I didn't know what I needed. Sure would have been nice to know what I didn't know ahead of time — I'd most likely never have started.

Several months have now gone by and this thing now goes down the road quickly and safely, but it still looks like Hades. The looks problem was partly cured when a Hertz rent-a-truck rear ended me at a downtown stoplight. Quite minor, actually, but the driver of the truck insisted that I take the Merc into the Hertz body shop for repairs. I picked the car up two days or so later and couldn't believe my eyes — from the doors back, I had a new 1939 Merc convertible. New tail lights, bumper and bumperettes, trunk handle and lock, and shiny black paint. Wow!

But now the front half looked so scabby I was shamed into doing the front. It all takes time and money, and if I remember correctly I was now up to $45 per week, which was five and a half days. After about six months' ownership, though, and barely keeping my butt out of debtors' prison, the car looks good and runs really well. Tires have been replaced as deals came along, and the only real problem is the top, the header bar in particular. It was finger-jointed at the centre of the windshield and was a compound curve as well. The original I believe was oak, but I built one out of spruce — not as fancy as the original, but it at least held the screws for the side rails.

I can't remember if the top was supposed to be powered or not [Author's note: it wasn't]. I just remember having to have a friend help on one side while I was on the other to raise or lower it. It never got new fabric while I owned it but sure needed it.

The only mechanical problem I had with the car in the time I owned it was the transmission. Went through three of them in about a year. I actually got quite good at dropping the rear end and torque tube after the first time. Thanks again for Hot Wrench.

I traded the car in at Ted Davy's car lot on the Danforth for a 1951 Plymouth two-door hardtop. Bad move! I drove the Plymouth for about a month and got tired of everybody blowing my doors off. That flathead I built had spoiled me, also I wanted another ragtop.

The Plymouth and another $400 (thanks, Mom) got me my first of seven 1951 Mercury convertibles. The last one I drove for thirty-four years and sold it two years ago.

My wife of forty-three years and I have almost constantly had a convertible, and along with the Mercs have been a couple of Austin-Healeys, an A-40 Jensen body Austin, a Corvair, a 1964 Ford, a 1970 TR6, an MGA and B, and our present summer driver, a 1969 Chrysler Newport that still has its original green vinyl/nylon top, about 95 percent perfect.

My present restoration project is a 1956 Lincoln Premier convertible. The majority of work has been done and paid for, and it's going back together slowly — feel like I did when I owned the 1939 Merc — wish I knew what I was doing.

I was the founding president of the Lakehead Antique Car Club in 1961-1962-1963 and owned a Model A Ford touring in conjunction with my brothers-in-law and a 1929 A roadster, 1927 T roadster pickup, and 1922 Durant touring.

Lots of cars over the years, but the first convertible, like your first sweetheart, holds a special place in your heart.

CHAPTER SEVEN:

BOB KIRK'S 1956 BUICK CENTURY: THE TIRE-SQUEALING SUMMER OF 1966 IN WHITBY, ONTARIO *By Bob Kirk*

Don't I look like trouble ready to happen at any moment? Well, in those days I was, and usually at the wide end of the bat! That's me, Bob Kirk, eighteen years old and driving a car a little too big for me at the time. The car was a 1956 Buick Century, and although it is missing in the picture, it had four portholes on the side of the front fenders, a definite sign of distinction. And me, I was about 110 pounds in this picture, but when I was behind the wheel of this brute of a car, I had an attitude of someone much larger and tougher. I couldn't begin to tell you of the many times I got myself into trouble with this car and this attitude. It was a fast car, and I could usually outrun most of the problems I got into.

Once the neighbours called the police complaining about my wild driving, dragging and squealing tires. Then they called my parents to tell them that they had called the police. My mum told me, and I quickly grabbed the garden hose and started to wash my car just as the police arrived.

"I'm sorry, Officer," I said, "it must have been another car similar to mine."

"With the name 'The Banshee' on the fenders?" the policeman replied. "We will be watching for this car," he firmly stated. I also used this tank for a tow truck a few times to pull my buddies' cars out of ditches and creeks, etc. Fifty or so cars, and thirty-eight years, later, I still think of this car and miss it, although I don't miss the trouble it caused.

CHAPTER EIGHT

HAZLETT AND JONES — USED CAR SALES By Gord Hazlett

Gord Hazlett of Toronto is a retired auto mechanic with fifty years in the trade. He now writes a regular column for Old Autos *newspaper. His hilarious stories, drawn from true life experience, have delighted readers across Canada for more than a decade. Gord is also the proud author of three books that form a permanent collection of his wonderful stories. The following story appeared on page 46 of his first book,* Old Auto Tales.

Years ago, before the war, around 1938, used cars were a dime a dozen, I got that saying from Mulroney, and very hard to sell. The lots on the Danforth were full, and to cover the rent and hydro bills, they would wholesale a few cars off the back row to the wreckers around the end of the month. Mitch Forbes, owner of Greenwood Auto Wreckers, used to get quite a few of these gems as he was the biggest and closest wrecker and also always paid a fair price and in spot cash. This, the shyster car dealers liked. On one such deal there was a 1930 Chrysler four-door sedan, maroon in colour, and what we called a Greenwood resale. Too good to wreck. Now my story.

There was another shyster who hung around the wreckers like a vulture waiting for something to come in that he could make a fast buck on. His name was Fred Jones; I can say this as Jonesy, as we called him, passed away many years ago. Another thing I might mention about Jonesy is he *always* wore a bowler hat and a suit coat with his discharge button from the First War in his lapel. It sure was an odd way to dress for someone to hang around the wreckers. I supposed he wanted to look like a big operator. Well, sir, Jonesy spotted this Chrysler and he knew someone wanting such a car. He asked Mitch how much he wanted for it, and if my memory serves me right, I believe it was $125. Jonesy phones this fellow up, his name was Malaney and he operated a garage on Parliament Street, told him to get over to the wreckers right away as he had this gem waiting just for him for only $125. While waiting for Malaney to appear, Mitch went out and took another look at the Chrysler and figured it should be worth $150. Well, when Malaney came over to look at the car, Jonesy had to tell him about the extra $25. Malaney got so upset that he wouldn't even look at the car. He called Jonesy and Mitch a few names I won't tell you and stomped out to his car and took off.

Gord Hazlett's first car was this 1923 Model T coupe purchased for $10 in 1936 and sold two years later for $11. Posing for the photo were Gord's friend Bill Reid on the deck lid, brother Tom in the driver's seat, and brother John on the hood.

Of course, Jonesy was mad at losing a possible sale as he worked on some sort of commission deal with Mitch. He stewed about this for about a week and I guess Mitch took pity on him and finally said it was okay to sell it to Malaney for $125. Right away Jonesy phones Malaney the good news, but Malaney was still mad and said he wouldn't buy the car at any price after the price hike caper Mitch pulled. Jonesy let it bother him for another week, then cooked up this scheme to sell Malaney the car. Enter Gord Hazlett.

At my home on Ashdale Avenue there was a former stable made into a three-car garage in the yard. The idea was to put the Chrysler in one of these garages, call Malaney, and tell him he, Jonesy, found another Chrysler just like the one he was looking for at a fellow's house on Ashdale Ave. He phoned Malaney to come and see it. As I said before, this car was maroon and you know how they used to fade, well, Jonesy saw a drain pan with some old oil in it, so while waiting for Malaney to arrive, he soaked a rag in the old oil and went over the whole car with it. I'm telling you it looked like it just came out of the paint shop. Malaney didn't know me from Adam so the car was supposed to be mine that I was selling due to hard times. Jonesy was the big-hearted guy that was trying to help me out. When Malaney asked me the price and before I could get my mouth open, Jonesy says $175. The car was started to hear the motor and backed out into the daylight for a better look.

Malaney bought the car. It just goes to show you how a little used oil, a few white lies, and a lot of blarney can sell a car, if you had the nerve, and Jonesy sure had. I found out later he only paid Mitch $125, and all I got out of the deal was a 20-cent package of Ogdens fine cut and a very guilty conscience.

For my younger readers, if any, car dealing was so simple in those days. Two bucks for a transfer, no insurance, no certifying, no PST, GST, there I go crying about the old days.

Here's a recent photo of Gord in the middle flanked by the Old Car Detective (right) and Bob Chapman (left), whose 1931 Chrysler roadster was featured in 60 Years Behind the Wheel.

CHAPTER NINE:

ED SMITH'S 1956 STUDEBAKER OVER FORTY YEARS AGO *By Ed Smith*

On March 11, 2004, the following letter arrived from Ed Smith in Vineland, Ontario.

Dear Bill,

I enjoyed your first edition of *60 Years Behind the Wheel* immensely, and it inspired me to dig up an old photo that I had in a family album. The photo shows my brother, Duncan Smith, and myself, Ed Smith, standing by my 1956 Studebaker Champion. The photo was taken in 1964. The car was not a chick magnet (neither were my brother or I), but it did give great service in transporting several of us from McMaster University to St. Catharines. At the time I charged each passenger fifty cents per ride to help cover gas. The car had a flathead six-cylinder motor and a three-speed shift on the column (three on the tree, as we used to say). It burned some oil and STP oil treatment was a regular addition at oil change time. Looking at this photo sure brought back memories.

CHAPTER TEN:

PUMPING GAS OVER FORTY YEARS AGO

I originally wrote this story for the January 20, 1992, issue of Old Autos *newspaper under the title "Pumping Gas 30 Years Ago."*

My brief but exciting career in the gasoline business began in Toronto on New Year's Day in 1962. I was nineteen at the time and in my first year at York University. My Chevy-powered 1940 Mercury convertible was laid up for the winter in my parents' garage, and I was bombing around town in my mom's navy blue 1961 Pontiac V8 two-door hardtop (the model with the big rear window and the first car in our family to have the new narrow whitewall tires).

I had been up all night — from New Year's Eve till sunrise — helping a friend named Pete Clancy work on his Olds Rocket-powered 1939 Merc convertible. On my way home for breakfast, I pulled in for gas at Harold Lehman's Esso station at Bayview and Broadway and filled the tank of Mom's Pontiac with my last five-dollar bill. Premium gas back then was 44.9 cents a gallon and regular was 39.9. Now flat broke, I walked into the office and asked the man behind the counter for a part-time job. He took my name and number and said he would call me if any openings came up.

I didn't have long to wait. He phoned me around five o'clock the next day and told me to report for duty for the six-to-ten shift that night. I told him I was on my way.

I started pumping gas at 5:50 p.m. on what felt like the coldest night of the year. The next four hours were a nightmare. I had never pumped gas before (there were no self-serves back then), and I quickly learned there was more to pumping gas than just pumping gas.

Lehman's Esso at that time was pumping a million gallons a year from four pumps at the front and three at the side. One of the side pumps had no automatic shut-off (it hadn't been converted yet), and customers were not required to shut their engines off while getting gas. You could even smoke a cigarette within ten feet of the pumps, and some customers did.

The first car I served was a faded blue 1954 Ford sedan, and the driver wanted "two bucks of the cheap stuff." I smiled smugly as I lifted the nozzle off the pump and pulled the rear licence plate down to expose the gas cap. My mom and dad had owned a pair of 1954 Fords, and those were the two cars I learned to drive on. So I knew exactly where to put the gas in. But this guy's cap was frozen shut, and I couldn't budge it. Finally, I held the hose and nozzle between my legs (you can imagine what that looked like!) and had to use both my hands to get the cap unstuck.

Then I shoved the nozzle in and squeezed the handle. Nothing happened. I started to panic. Then I noticed I had forgotten to turn the pump back to $00.00 to erase the previous sale. I let go of the nozzle to flick the switch on the side of the pump, and that's when the nozzle popped out of the filler neck and fell into the snow. In my haste to put it back in before anyone saw it on the ground, I tripped over the hose and landed in the snow on my hands and knees. The driver began adjusting his rear-view mirror to see what was going on at the back of his car, and the car behind me backed up and went to another pump.

I finally got the gas flowing into his tank, then couldn't remember how much he had asked for. "Did you want it filled up?" I yelled. I wasn't going to leave the hose to walk up to his door. Unfortunately, his window was rolled up (it was the middle of winter) and he couldn't hear me. He finally heard me on the third yell and held up two fingers. (I can imagine which finger would have gone up if he had wanted only one dollar.)

In my first hour on the job, I had to find gas filler caps in every place imaginable. On the 1956 Chevy, you had to turn a section of the left tail light to get at it. On the 1957 Chevy, it was hidden behind the left tail fin. On the 1958 Chevy, the gas cap flap was cleverly camouflaged in a section of the body between the trunk lid and the rear bumper. The 1959 Chevy had it behind the rear licence plate, just like the 1954 Ford. I wondered why the designers at Chevrolet couldn't make up their minds where to put it.

At 7:00 p.m., all the other gas stations in the area closed up because of a City of Toronto by-law.

More than thirty years after I pumped gas at Harold Lehman's Esso station, I found this clear-vision Esso pump at the Barrie Automotive Swap Meet. It was too big to fit into the trunk of my 1947 Mercury 114 convertible, so I brought home this photo of it instead.

And that's when our station really got busy. All of a sudden, cars pulled in from all directions and lined up at the pumps five or six deep. And that's when the boss — Harold Lehman — rolled up in his red and white 1960 Buick four-door sedan to give us a hand and keep us on our toes. He barked orders left and right and soon discovered I was new on the job.

I quickly learned we were selling oil as well as gas. And you couldn't sell any oil unless you got under the hood first. I made the mistake of saying to one customer at the height of the rush, "The oil's all right tonight, sir?" The man shrugged and said, "I guess so …" Then he drove off. Harold had been standing right behind me when I said this, and when I turned around, he was fuming! "How do you know the oil's all right unless you check it first!"

But if I was a little slow that night, some of our customers were even slower. Ross Peacock was very proud of his sparkling white 1956 Olds convertible with the spinner wheel discs, and he always pulled up to the pumps super-slow to remind us to slow down and give him our very best attention.

Just after he left, a guy pulled up in a very rusty 1956 Dodge sedan with the engine clattering. He bought fifty cents' worth of gas, then told me to check the oil. The dipstick was bone dry! I showed it to him, and he said he would add some oil the next time he was in for gas. By this time, his girlfriend had climbed out, shut the hood, and slid back in beside him. They drove off with his engine still clattering and me still holding his dipstick.

The rest of the evening was a blur. "Three dollars of hi-test and make it snappy." "I think you better check my tires." "Don't use that oily rag on my windshield!" "I need the key to the washroom." "Could you check my antifreeze?" "One of my headlights is burned out." "I can't get my trunk open. The lock's frozen." My worst mistake of the evening was putting five bucks' worth of gas into a car, then having the customer insist he had only asked for two. I had to use a rubber hose and gas can to siphon out the three bucks. And that's when I got a mouthful of gasoline.

When my shift ended at ten, I thought for sure I was going to get fired. Harold pointed a finger at me and said, "Go into the office and tell Jimmy to give you all the extra hours he can 'cause you need the practice real bad!"

CHAPTER ELEVEN:

THE SHERK BROTHERS BUY A 1937 BUICK

My brother John and I bought a 1937 Buick Special four-door sedan for $50 in our home-town of Leamington, Ontario, in the summer of 1961. Lefty Liddle, a university student, was selling it, and John and I went to Lefty's home on Howard Avenue to look at it. I noticed the speedometer needle was stuck at 110 miles per hour, and that right there sold me on the car. Where else could you buy a fifty-dollar car that would go that fast?

At first, Lefty couldn't get it running. He fixed it later that day and phoned us. My brother and I each kicked in $25 from our summer jobs (we were still in school), and I picked up the car from Lefty at Erie Produce near the north end of town, where he was working that summer. What a car! The hood was half a block long, and the car had running boards!

The very next day I loaded the entire back seat with Model A Ford car parts and headed for our home in Toronto. Five miles east of Wheatley, the back seat caught on fire. I pulled over to the side of the highway, emptied all the parts from the back seat — it looked like a wrecking yard had exploded — yanked out the burning floor carpet and lower half of the back seat, and held them under water in the irrigation ditch at the side of the highway.

Then I examined the cause of the fire. The tailpipe had already rotted off before we bought the car, and the hot exhaust gases were coming out of the muffler and up through a rust hole in the floor. That set the floor carpet on fire, and it spread to the back seat. I left the carpet in the ditch (it's probably still there), re-installed the back seat, re-loaded all the car parts right up to the ceiling, and I was on my way again.

About fifty miles further down Highway 3, I was barrelling along at about 60 miles per hour. Suddenly I heard a loud *bang* right under the car. It sounded like a hand grenade. I glanced in my rear-view mirror and saw my muffler bouncing end over end into the ditch on the other side of the highway, narrowly missing the Volkswagen behind me. I stepped on the gas and kept going.

A hundred miles later I was on Highway 5 approaching the edge of Hamilton Mountain. It began pouring rain, and I couldn't find the switch for the windshield wipers, so I straightened both legs and squeezed my head and shoulders out through the driver's window and drove for twenty miles with the wind and rain in my face.

I finally got to Toronto and was driving along the Lakeshore when the starter motor came on and began grinding itself to pieces against the ring gear on the flywheel. I got as far as a parking lot on Wellington Street in downtown Toronto before it jammed up completely. I climbed out, opened my tool box, crawled under the car, unbolted the starter motor, and carried it on my lap on a Toronto streetcar about ten or fifteen blocks to a repair shop.

Two hours later they finished rebuilding it, and I took the streetcar back to my car. I bolted the starter motor back onto the side of the engine and pressed down on the gas pedal. The engine started right up — and so did the grinding noise all over again! I drove as slowly as I could back to the repair shop (it wouldn't grind under 10 miles per hour). The man there pointed to another repair shop further down the street and told me to ask for a fellow named Axel.

I got a hold of Axel, who, in his broken English, indicated that I should lift the hood on the driver's side. The starter motor was on the other side, so I'm thinking, *Oh, no, this guy knows less about cars than I do.* I was wrong. He reached in and disconnected a rod attached at one end to the accelerator linkage, then, pulling on that rod, he revved up the engine with no grinding! He refused to accept any payment, and he waved me on my way.

Now I'm heading north up University Avenue, past Queen's Park, past the Royal Ontario Museum, and I'm entering the intersection at Avenue Road and Bloor when I hear something fall off the front of my car, and then I ran over it. I pulled over after clearing the intersection, climbed out, and looked to see if I was missing something.

I was. The front licence plate had fallen off, and I had run over it. It was still in the middle of the intersection, and now other cars were running over it too. I waited for the lights to change, then ran out, picked it up, tossed it into the back seat, and continued on my way.

Now I was heading north to our house. I headed up Yonge Street past Eglinton, past Castlefield, past Glengrove, and turned left at Chatsworth Crescent, a one-way going west. And that's when a police cruiser pulled me over.

He parked behind me and walked up to the old 1937 Buick to tell me my front licence plate was missing. I reached into the back seat and showed him the plate and promised I would reattach it tomorrow morning. He said okay and walked back to his cruiser.

We were parked on a hill, and he was behind me. I waited for him to leave so I could roll backwards down the hill to get my car started by pulling the rod beside the engine. I waited and waited, but he didn't leave. Finally I decided to ask for his help in getting me out of there.

I walked back to his cruiser and explained that I could only start the car from under the hood and the car had to be in neutral — but my emergency brake didn't work and I didn't want to roll backwards and smash into his cruiser. Would he mind holding my bumper jack under my rear wheels until I got my car started, and then throw the jack in through an open window as I pulled away? Believe it or not, he did. And as I headed up the hill and away, I had to really step on the gas — and that's when he would have realized I had no muffler. The engine sounded like a machine gun, but he let me go.

Part of the car had already been damaged before John and I bought it. Lefty's older brother had been driving it through the traffic circle at Stoney Creek near Hamilton when another car smashed into the right rear door. This was in the days before the Burlington Skyway. The door looked mangled, but it still opened and closed and the window still went up and down.

In September 1961, John and I were back in school in Toronto, and we decided to sell the 1937 Buick. We ran an ad in the *Toronto Star*, and the owner of a pawnshop on Queen Street East bought it for $75. To close the deal, I agreed to drive it to his country property a few miles north of Toronto and park it in his barn. This I did, and I never saw it again.

Leamington Post & News, *Thursday, July 8, 1937.*

YOU'LL BE *Out in front* **IN THIS BLUE-RIBBON WINNER**

IF you want a whole lot more than ordinary motoring — at just a very little more than ordinary cost — McLaughlin-Buick's your car!

It's a thoroughbred; thirty years of building back of it, years and years of blue-ribbon performance in front of it. It's a beauty; the most distinctive, most exciting-looking fine car of the year. It's built for *action*. You'll be riding high — on the crest of the wave — when it's yours!

Make it yours today . . . the McLaughlin-Buick you've always wanted. Come in and take a look at this year's fine "Special Series" models — lower priced, probably, than you ever thought McLaughlin-Buicks might be. But that's just the natural result of three decades of McLaughlin-Buick leadership . . . a *finer* car for *less* money.

PRICED FROM **$1207**

(SERIES 44—SPORT COUPE WITH OPERA SEATS)

Delivered at factory, Oshawa. Government taxes, license and freight additional. (Prices subject to change without notice.)

Monthly payments to suit your purse on the General Motors Instalment Plan.

M-1878

MᶜLAUGHLIN-BUICK

Ray A. Young CORNER ERIE AND MILL STS. B-A. Service Station; Phone 359 LEAMINGTON

CHAPTER TWELVE

BOB JAMES REMEMBERS HIS 1941 FORD CONVERTIBLE

It was a September day in 1952, and Bob James was driving along Decarie Boulevard in Montreal in his very first car: a dark blue 1938 Plymouth coach. (See page 118.) He was eighteen years old and itching for something more exciting to drive around town to impress all the girls.

Suddenly, from the corner of his eye, he spotted a 1941 Ford Super Deluxe convertible parked on the used car lot of Decarie Motors. He pulled in for a closer look — and it was love at first sight.

This yellow ragtop had maroon fenders, a fancy grille guard, headlight eyebrows, an aftermarket hood ornament, and flashy gobs of extra chrome on both front fenders. Bob walked slowly around it, drinking in all the details. He looked inside and noticed that the maroon leather interior harmonized nicely with the fenders and the hand-painted maroon dashboard. It still had the original radio, and the power top still worked.

Pride of ownership is all over Bob James' face in this hairy-chested view of his pride and joy. Note the crank-hole in the grille and the stick-on window tint at the top of the windshield. This photo was taken in the parking lot at the beach on Lake Champlain in Plattsburgh, New York, less than a day's drive from his home in Montreal.

The sticker price was $495, and Bob just had to have it. He used his 1938 Plymouth as a trade-in (worth $245) and agreed to pay the $250 balance in twelve monthly instalments of $27 each. Then they handed him the keys, and Bob drove off, the proud new owner.

The engine burned oil, and Bob could smell the fumes inside the car, even with the top down. He bought his oil in bulk (#50) and slanted the vent windows way back for extra fresh air. Bob also bought an aftermarket oil cap for the engine with a flexible hose to divert the fumes under the car.

He installed an *aaoogah!* horn, which served as a wolf whistle whenever he spotted pretty girls walking along the street. Then he shaved the rear deck and moved the licence plate down onto the rear bumper, giving the car a big, round, smooth-looking rear end.

Bob couldn't resist mounting a spare tire on the trunk lid, a popular fad at the time, when every cool guy with a convertible just had to have a continental kit to add extra flash to the rear end. Bob bought a spare tire with metal cover and mounting bracket off a 1936 Ford sedan at an auto wreckers and removed it himself in the wrecking yard.

The holes in the trunk lid were drilled at Hart Motors, a Mercury-Lincoln-Meteor dealer where Bob's dad worked. With the continental kit now on the car, Bob couldn't open the trunk because the outside spare was hitting the rear bumper.

No problem. Bob moved the rear bumper back several inches, and while he was doing this he decided to replace both stock bumpers with the sexy-looking ribbed bumpers off a 1949 Plymouth. He got these from a wrecking yard in Granby, Quebec, for five dollars. And it was Bob's idea to do this. Very few car magazines were available back then, and you had to rely upon your own creativity in customizing your car.

Now Bob could open the trunk, but it wouldn't stay open because the lid was too heavy. No problem. Bob used an iron bar to keep it propped up, thereby removing the risk of being decapitated or having his back broken.

A proud eighteen-year-old Bob James sits behind the wheel of his newly purchased 1941 Ford convertible in Montreal in September 1952. Note the unusual hood ornament and fender trim and the two-tone paint, especially on the upper part of the door, foreshadowing the door trim on 1956 Mercurys.

All this work on the rear end probably gave Bob his next idea. He installed a wire and switch under the dash to turn off his rear licence plate light in case he was ever being chased by the police. And Bob was quick to point out this feature to any girls who were riding in his car. The nice girls usually jumped out

at the next stoplight, but the girls who liked to ride on the wild side of life usually moved closer to Bob.

After driving the car a few months, Bob got tired of the admittedly tacky yellow and maroon colour scheme and had the car repainted "Banff Blue," a popular 1951 Meteor colour. Hart Motors did the repaint. Bob's dad, George James, worked as a clerk in the service department and spread the cost of Bob's paint job across the servicing of several army vehicles. The Korean War was still on at this time, and Hart Motors had the contract to refurbish mobile hospital vehicles that had been left in Holland after the Second World War and brought back to Canada for sandblasting and repainting. In other words, the paint job on Bob's car was free. (And you wonder why our taxes are so high!)

What a difference! Bob has now repainted the car "Banff Blue" with wide whitewalls, 1949 Plymouth ribbed bumpers, and a fancy hood ornament ready to "fly off."

While Bob had been doing all the work on his rear end, he had no way of knowing that he would also have to work on his front end. He was driving home one day from the Goodyear Tire head office at 2050 Cote de Liesse Road, where he worked. The traffic was bumper to bumper, and just ahead of Bob was a big stake truck. It had no brake lights, so Bob smashed into it. Then he pulled off the road to check the damage while the truck drove off. Bob phoned his dad, who sent a tow truck to bring him to Hart Motors. The hood, grille, and left front fender were damaged (see photo).

All the front end sheet metal was removed by Bob and his friends, but Bob needed the car to get to work. He drove it back and forth to work for several days with no front fenders and hood. Hart Motors did all the body work while Bob went to Vincent's Auto Wreckers in Ville St. Pierre, where he picked up a used hood, grille, and left front fender. These had come off a red 1941 Ford, and Bob had to drive around for a couple of weeks with a red hood and red front fender on his "Banff Blue" ragtop before the car could be brought back for repaint. The new (used) hood did not fit as well as the old one, and it popped open once between installation and repaint, but Bob was able to see between the hood and the cowl well enough to pull off the road. Finally the front end was repainted, and because the paint on the rest of the car was only a few months old, matching it was easy.

Incredible as it may sound, Bob still has *all* the receipts for all the work done on his 1941 Ford during the year and a half that he owned it — from September 1952 to March 1954. In fact, Bob has all the receipts for all the cars he has ever owned.

Here is a sampling of the receipts for his 1941 Ford:

On September 15, 1952, (two days after he bought the car), Bob had Hart Motors check the front end to make sure the car was safe to drive. Cost: $3.38. No certification required back then.

On September 30, Bob visited Lorne Kidd's Esso gas station in Montreal West for "a cable and housing, fan belt, 2 lbs. of gear oil for trans. and diff., and a part for gearshift linkage." The bill (including tax and labour) came to $14.18.

To save wear and tear on the floor of his new ragtop, Bob went to International Harvester Co., where he worked for a year and a half in the stockroom, on September 30 (the same day he went to Lorne Kidd's Esso) and spent $3.15 on a floor mat (part #999859R1).

Anxious to hear Christmas carols on his car radio, Bob visited Edwards Electric at 5362 Sherbrooke Street West on December 24, 1952 to purchase a six-inch speaker for $8.80 ("Deck the halls…").

On January 30, 1953, Bob went to his local Handy Andy store and bought, among other things, a hammer, a funnel, pliers, sandpaper, and a bulb ($8.79). On the back of the receipt are these words: "Hold On To This Sales Slip."

Monday, September 14, 1953, was a happy day for Bob because that's when he made his last payment on the 1941 Ford. The car was now all his.

And just in time too. Less than a month later, Bob had his aforementioned accident with the stake truck. This led to an October 10, 1953, visit to Ville St. Pierre Automobile Service at 101 Elm Avenue, where Bob purchased a replacement hood ($15), grille ($12), and left fender ($3). That plus one used rad on exchange ($21) brought the total to $61.

Now back to Hart Motors for the body work and installation of all those replacement parts. That bill came to $74.33. The odometer on Bob's car by that time was showing 74,150 miles.

Early in 1954, Bob's car wouldn't shift into third gear, and once again Hart Motors came to the rescue. Only $7.16 worth of parts were needed, and this bill with labour came to $29.81.

Soon after that was fixed, Bob's dad phoned him to come quick to Hart Motors to see the car that just came in as a trade-in on a new Mercury. It was a very rare wood-bodied 1947 Ford Sportsman convertible, and it was up for sale for $700.

Bob rushed right down and bought it. He drove it for two years, then sold it in 1956. Forty-seven years later, the full story of that car appeared in my book *60 Years Behind the Wheel*.

It could have been worse. Instead of flying through the windshield with no seat belt, Bob faced only some minor body work after hitting the rear of a stake truck that had no brake lights.

CHAPTER THIRTEEN

OLD CAR STORIES AT WHEATLEY BAPTIST CHURCH

In his younger days, Pastor Klaus Hildebrandt (front right) and three pals were photographed while examining the internal workings of this 1934 Pontiac in British Columbia in the 1950s.

My old car buddy Bill "Wizard" Derbyshire invited me to attend the Wheatley Baptist Church on Sunday, January 25, 2004, to talk about old cars. The service of worship would begin at 11:00 a.m. followed by a delicious buffet luncheon of chicken and salad and dessert catered by the Car Barn Restaurant. Then I would be handed a microphone and turned loose. I said yes.

In no time at all, the appointed day arrived, and the church limo (a.k.a. John and Liese Sabelli's GM van) picked me up at our front door and got me to the church on time. As soon as I settled into a pew, I felt right at home because up by the altar was a giant screen displaying one old car photo after another — so big they were larger than life. And over the PA system could be heard two of the greatest old car songs of all time: "The Car" by Jeff Carson and "Riding With Private Malone" by David Ball.

Suddenly the title of the sermon filled the screen: "Hitching a Ride on a Chariot." Pastor Klaus Hildebrandt delivered an inspiring address in which he asked the congregation what kind of car Jesus would drive if He were here on earth today. Klaus suggested the Honda Accord, based on a passage in the Bible describing Jesus and his disciples as "being of one accord."

After lunch, I swung into action. I briefly outlined my work as an "old car detective," then invited people to come forward and share their old car memories with us. The first volunteer to reach the microphone was the pastor himself, Klaus Hildebrandt, and his automotive memories proved to be highly entertaining.

"I was the guy in Vancouver who drove the first Volkswagen. It wasn't my own car. It belonged to a friend of mine, but my friend got a job at a logging camp so he couldn't drive the car up the mountains, and he asked me to look after his Volkswagen. He had the first Volkswagen in British Columbia and the seventh Volkswagen sold on the North American continent. I drove that car to look after it, and I had all kinds of fun. It was really something.

"Let me just tell you a short story. I was on the ferry going across the Fraser River — now they have a bridge there. I had the Volkswagen parked on the ferry, and an American came along, a rich big shot, and he had his Chrysler parked on the other side. I saw him step out of the Chrysler and then he walked over to my Volkswagen and he looked at it and he lifted up the hood in the back — he apparently knew something about cars — and then shook his head and slammed it shut.

Pastor Klaus owned and drove this 1937 Chevy four-door sedan in British Columbia in the 1950s. He's the one behind the wheel.

And I thought to myself, *If you can do that to my car, I can do it to your car too*, and I walked up to his Chrysler and I opened the hood and I looked at his engine and I shook my head and I slammed it shut. And the guy gave me a dirty look. He didn't agree with that kind of treatment of his car.

"Let me tell you another short story about a 1928 Model A. A big square thing. If you are ever called in to do your driver's licence or road test again, make sure you buy a 1928 Model A Ford. In my happy bachelor days, I mean, I'm still happy [hearty laughter], my wife is here, I enjoy married life too, but in my happy bachelor days, in those days when I was still young and kind of crazy, for sixty-five bucks — a friend of mine made me aware of it — a Model A was for sale in Richmond, B.C., south of Vancouver. So for sixty-five bucks, I bought this Model A, rented a garage, and started to renovate the thing. Now the only thing I really needed for it were kingpins for the steering, and I thought, where would I get those? I decided to check out the Ford dealer — the biggest Ford dealer in town. And I asked, where would I get kingpins? And he said, 'Of course, here. We are the Ford dealer. We have all the parts for a Model A Ford. We could build a complete car if we wanted to, just by pulling the parts off the shelf, but it would get much too expensive.' But the kingpins he provided were just the right thing for that car. The only thing I ended up having problems with was the frame for the windshield. I could never get one like that and I had to just patch it up and tape it over. But I had lots of fun.

"And then the B.C. government called me in to do my driver's licence and road test again. In those days you had to do it every six or seven years, so I decided to drive there, downtown, in my Model A Ford. I parked it on the parking lot, went in, and came back out with the examiner, the guy who tests you, and he said, 'Which one is your car?' And I said 'The big black square one. The one over in the corner.' And he said, 'You mean you came down here in that Model A Ford to do your road test?' And I said 'Yes, why not? It's safety-tested and everything, it's got mechanical brakes, very reliable.' Those brakes, by the way, were wonderful brakes because they always took care of the pedestrians when they were crossing the street. I just had to hit my mechanical brakes and they went *Screech! Screech! Screech!* — and you should have seen the pedestrians run for their lives [howls of laughter].

"And the examiner said, 'If you drove that old car down here with double-clutching and the lever for the spark advance, you know how to drive and you don't have to take the test.' Then he said, 'I haven't been in one of these old cars in years and I'd like to have a little joy ride. Could you take me around the block?'

"Well, I just had to. Then he could mark on his paper that he had actually tested me. I told him I'd be happy to take him around the block. That's all he asked for. So I drove him around the block.

"One hour later we were still driving around the streets in downtown Vancouver. He enjoyed it so much, he took the wheel eventually and drove the car himself, and he had a very pleasant afternoon with me and enjoyed that drive.

"For three years, from 1959 to 1962, I drove that car to youth meetings. The ignition didn't work, it was worn out, and you could start the car with any key, but there was a little secret I had. There was a tap under the dash, and you could turn the gas off.

"I was a member of the Young People's group in Vancouver at that time, and the young people knew that the ignition didn't work. What they didn't know was that there was a tap under the dash. And so sometimes after a youth meeting or church service, they would take off in my car, and then, to their frustration, the car would go *putt-putt-putt* about three houses down the road and would stop. And they could never understand how I got that car restarted.

"I had lots of fun, drove it for three years, even to work, then, it's a sad thing, after three years I sold it for a hundred and fifty bucks. That was around 1962, I wish I still had it."

At that point (and amid spirited applause), Klaus surrendered the microphone and returned to his seat. I blathered on for a few minutes about some of my all-time favourite old car stories, then asked for more volunteers from the audience.

Bud Foster came forward to share some automotive memories. Bud is a retired auto mechanic and brought with him a photo of an old brass-rad Model T touring. The photo was taken around 1917.

"I don't know too much about this car. I never saw it, but my wife's relative, Mr. Dales, worked for the Cockshutt dealership here in town where the theatre used to be. It was just a big old barn, and I can remember at Saturday night concerts, he would be standing there in the doorway, and I was just a little kid, and he had a Cockshutt horse plough right in the doorway for everyone to see. I've worked on these Model T's. I was a mechanic, and I tell everybody I've worked on Model T's, Cadillacs, manure spreaders, combines, diesel tractors, chainsaws, you name it, also diesel International trucks. The best job was chainsaws. I loved working on those. They're real easy to handle, eh? I went from a big International truck garage where you had a big hydraulic jack to pick up the radiators and fenders off a truck to a Toyota, and I picked up that radiator with two fingers. It was a real shock to go from one to the other.

"My uncle, Jack Brown, was an engineer in Detroit. He was walking down the street one Sunday morning with another engineer, and Henry Ford came driving along with his car. It wasn't a Model T because the flywheel went around laying flat — one of his first cars. And it stopped in front of where Uncle Jack was walking, and Henry Ford said, 'Jack, come and give me a shove to get me going.' Henry and his wife were in this car, all homemade put together, and they walked over and gave him a push, and Uncle Jack said to Henry, 'Why don't you quit your fiddlin' around and make a living like the rest of us?' And Henry said, 'Jack, I'm going to make a million out of this.' And that's exactly what happened."

I then carried the mike over to a table set up at the front, where people were displaying old photos of old cars brought from home. The first one I picked up showed a 1937 Chevrolet four-door sedan. I asked who'd brought in this photo, and it turned out to be Pastor Klaus Hildebrandt for a return engagement at the microphone.

"I didn't know I would get another chance to speak, but some preachers do get a second chance. Let me introduce my 1937 Chevy. It had a six-cylinder straight engine, suicide doors with rear doors opening from the front, and the reason I bought the car — I spent 1955 and 1957 in Kelowna, British Columbia, trying to make a living there, not realizing that most work in Kelowna is seasonal. That's why I ended up working for a golf course and a packing house and all kinds of jobs — whatever I could get a hold of. Lo and behold, the packing house burned down and I found myself without a job. For three months I was unemployed and, for the first time in Canada, I drew unemployment insurance. Life was so sweet and cheap in Kelowna that I could actually buy a car with my unemployment money. And so for a hundred dollars, I bought this 1937 Chevy. It was green — not the original colour — and it was a wonderful car.

"It was a bit slow in starting in the morning, especially on a cold morning. It went *r-r-r-r-roar*! I thought, *Maybe I might have to buy a battery for this car. If it breaks down after half a year, I really haven't lost anything because the depreciation is nothing when you pay a hundred dollars for a car.*

"One of the most wonderful stories with that car was when I ended up the wrong way on a Greyhound bus depot. For some reason, I drove in onto the platform. I didn't realize it at the moment, but the car was so high and so long, you couldn't always see what was coming. And all of a sudden, I reached the edge of the platform and *thud!* The front wheels dropped about two feet down. It sank, you know. All of a sudden, you had that sinking feeling. I realized I had somehow come off the Greyhound platform onto one of the bus bays where the buses pull in to let the passengers out. The front end was down and the rear end was up, and I thought, *How do I get out of here before they fine me or get me?* I decided to put the car in reverse and give it all it had. And I really hit the gas hard and let the clutch come out — and sure enough, the car bounced back to life and pulled the front wheels up on that platform, and I drove away.

"I drove that car for a whole year, and the most expensive repair I had on it was when I came back from a trip to Kamloops — 116 miles — and the moment I pulled in, back in Kelowna, into the driveway of a friend's house, all of a sudden the car wouldn't go anymore. For some reason the speedometer still showed some mileage, but when I hit the gas it didn't go. Then I stepped out and noticed that one of the rear wheels had broken off!

"We decided to check the junk dealers, and sure enough they had a slightly used rear axle, and with the help of a mechanic friend, we put the rear axle back in and the car was repaired. The whole repair cost $1.75, and it worked. The axle held.

"But after about a year I noticed that the clutch was giving up. You could actually use third gear like an automatic transmission. You would start the car up in third gear and it would slowly pick up speed, and I decided it was about time to trade it in. And so I shopped around and traded it for a 1947 Buick. Beautiful car. A heavy car. Over four thousand pounds, straight eight engine. I enjoyed driving it and they gave me a good trade-in for the old Chevy — $125. So actually I made money on that thing.

"The wonderful thing that happened next was, I took the Buick for a test drive out on the highway. And as soon as I came out of town, I saw a green car sitting to the right of the road, and there was a fellow running around the car and scratching his head. And when I came closer, I realized — hey! — he's got my old Chevy [howls of laughter]. The one I had just traded for $125.

"I stopped behind him and I said, 'Can I help you with anything?' Well he said, 'I don't know if you can help me, but just this morning I bought this old Chevy, and as soon as I drove it out of town the clutch gave out [more howls of laughter from the audience], and it doesn't go no more.'

"'Well,' I said, 'the best I can do is take you to the nearest gas station and maybe they have a tow truck and they can tow it in.' But I never told him that I was the former owner of that car and I had just traded it in." [Big round of applause for Klaus!]

Another car driven by Pastor Klaus in British Columbia in the 1950s was this Fiat Topolino ("little mouse").

CHAPTER FOURTEEN

RICHARD BUSSE'S 1953 METEOR CUSTOMLINE By Richard Busse

I purchased my 1953 Meteor Customline four-door in 1962 from Hat Auto Sales in Medicine Hat, Alberta, for $275. It was medium brown with a white top and had a chocolate brown interior with a white Ford fiftieth-anniversary steering wheel. It had a 255-cubic-inch Mercury flathead with a three-speed standard and was equipped with the Mercury style airplane dash!

For a mild custom job, I nosed and decked it, removed the bumperettes, and added dual Hollywood exhausts with chrome turn-down extensions. The paint was 1959 GM "Venetian Turquoise Metallic" with 1960 Buick full disc hubcaps. The Meteor performed well on the unofficial drag strip by the Goodyear plant. It even outpaced the Ford 272s and 292s that had automatic transmissions.

Standing by my car I am wearing my Turnkeys car club jacket. The crest was a 1935 Ford coupe with a Hemi (our club car). I dated my high school sweetheart, Donna, in this car, and we are still together with two children and three grandchildren. I am driving my sixteenth Ford, a late model Mustang convertible, but my favourite car was that neat little Meteor I drove in high school.

Medicine Hat had the Turnkeys, the Gas City Customs, the Charioteers, and the Coachmen. Our club president, Jerry Bennis, insisted all members drive in a safe and courteous manner, assist all motorists in distress, and drive seniors to the polls and blood donor clinics. This was done to improve the club image, as the public was suspicious of car clubs. We got permission from Premier Manning's Social Credit government to shut down the Trans-Canada Highway on a Sunday long weekend for the first drag races.

When the Turnkeys disbanded in 1965, all assets were sold and monies donated to Muscular Dystrophy.

CHAPTER FIFTEEN:

BILL "WIZARD" DERBYSHIRE'S FIRST CAR

It was a brand new red 1967 Ford Falcon with six cylinders and a stick shift. Wizard and his mom bought it from Freeway Ford in Tilbury (one of three dealerships owned by Peter Pocklington, owner of the Edmonton Oilers), near his hometown of Wheatley, Ontario.

Wizard slammed the car through the gears — but never when his mom was riding with him. However, she soon learned about his hard shifting. One day, she was making a right turn and the horn started honking. This happened on every right turn. Back to the dealer, and the problem was corrected.

Soon after that, the same problem again. Horn blowing on right turns. Back to the dealer again. They took the steering column all apart, then asked Mrs. Derbyshire if she had a teenage son who drove the car. The hard shifting had mangled the innards of the column. Back home, Mom and son had a talk — problem solved.

Wizard's mother (now ninety-nine) poses with pride behind the wheel of her brand new 1967 Ford Falcon two-door sport coupe.

But Wiz found other ways to push the car to its limits — and beyond. In the winter, he'd find an icy stretch of road, then deliberately fishtail the car into a spin or skid, then practise coming out of the skid (turn front wheels in direction of skid, easy on the brakes, etc.).

Bigger and bigger skids were the challenge, till one day he lost control of the car and ended up half into a ditch with a tire and wheel badly mangled. What to do? Can't tell Mom.

Then a brainstorm. He installed the spare, put the baffed tire in the trunk, and drove home. Mom never looked in the trunk, and the damaged wheel and tire disappeared when the car was traded in on a 1970 Pontiac with a V8 under the hood.

But while the Falcon was still in the family, Wizard practised his skill at four-wheel drifts through a gravel and dirt U-turn. Got pretty good at it too. In fact, downright perfect.

But it's no fun unless you share it with your friends. He loaded the car with all his pals to show them what he could do. But he forgot to allow for the extra weight and once again lost control of the car. He went into another four-wheel drift he couldn't get out of, and the car spun sideways into a sand bank. Didn't hurt the car but scared the daylights out of Wiz and his pals.

Today, Wizard bombs around in a beautiful sparkling blue 1963 split-window Corvette, an equally blue 1966 Acadian two-door hardtop, a 1955 Chevy pickup truck, and (until it burned up) an early 1990s sky blue Geo convertible affectionately known as the "Slick Racer."

This is what Wizard drives today: a sleek, tire-squealing 1963 split-window Corvette recently purchased in Arizona and now a familiar sight on the streets of Wheatley and Leamington in southwestern Ontario.

Wizard still slams through the gears, even when he's driving an automatic. He put the Acadian into reverse (by mistake) the first day he had it when he slammed from low to drive. He hit reverse at 40 miles per hour and the rear wheels locked for a split-second, then Wiz snapped it into drive. He did this twice. No damage done.

He still drives at a pretty good speed, and his mother (now a hearty nintey-nine) can't catch him because there's no overdrive on her wheelchair.

CHAPTER SIXTEEN:

THE FIRST CAR MIKE FILEY WANTED TO BUY

Toronto historian Mike Filey was a wartime baby born in Toronto on Saturday, October 11, 1941. When he celebrated his thirteenth birthday in the fall of 1954, the new 1955 cars had just come out with fresh styling that captured the heart of the car-buying public. For Mike, one new car stood out above all the rest — the 1955 Pontiac Laurentian two-door hardtop, and it had to be turquoise and white with wide whitewalls. *If I could buy a new car*, thought young Mike, *that's the car I would buy.*

Forty-one years later, Mike became the proud owner of a mint original 1955 Pontiac Laurentian two-door hardtop. And yes, it was (and still is) turquoise and white with wide whitewalls. Mike's wife, Yarmila, began searching for that exact car soon after Mike turned fifty in 1991 (and she didn't tell him she was looking for one!). Five years later, in the summer before he turned fifty-five, "Surprise!" There it was, parked in his driveway, and Yarmila handed him the keys.

Mike Filey waited more than forty years to slide behind the wheel of his dream car (this turquoise and white 1955 Pontiac Laurentian two-door hardtop) — and the smile on his face tells you the car was worth waiting for. If Mike could sing (and maybe he can), he might want to paraphrase "The World I Used to Know" (an old Jimmy Rodgers song): "Someday the car I used to see, will come around and call on me, then I will slide behind the wheel, because at last my dream is real."

The search for that car is quite a story in itself. But first, let's roll back the clock to the days when Mike was a young lad growing up in North Toronto.

The family moved into the area in August 1950, into a house at 30 Elvina Gardens, where Mike's mother still lives to this day (his dad passed away in 1965). The first car

Mike and Yarmila often display their dream car at the popular Thornhill Cruise Nights, held every Monday through the motoring season and hosted by the very entertaining "Honest Nate" Salter and his crew of Thornhill cruisers.

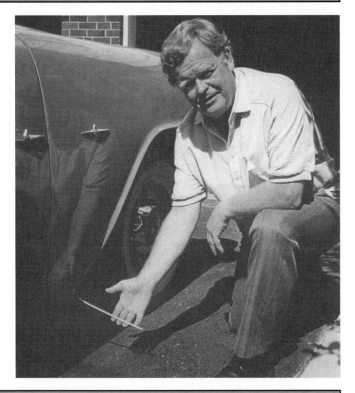

Mike is very proud of the wide whitewalls on his 1955 Pontiac. To protect them from scuff marks, he installed a set of "curb feelers," a popular accessory back in the 1950s.

Mike remembers his dad driving was a 1928 Pontiac named Min (maybe that's when Mike got hooked on this make). That was the first year that Pontiac had four-wheel brakes, and all cars so equipped back then carried a red metal triangle on the left rear fender to warn other drivers not to follow too close. The next car Mike remembers his dad driving was a DeSoto with a big outside sun visor and a fluid drive transmission.

Before Mike bought his first car (a 1949 Morris Minor), he spent his part-time money on model airplanes. He enjoyed soaking them with lighter fluid, then watching them crash-land in flames in the backyard.

When Mike entered Class 9B at North Toronto Collegiate in September 1955, the new 1955 Pontiacs had been on the road for nearly a year. He was not quite fourteen but was already madly in love with those Pontiacs — so much so, in fact, that he entered high school thinking, *Will I stay in school or drop out at sixteen and get a job so I can buy a 1955 Pontiac?*

He stayed in school.

After Mike passed his driver's test at age eighteen in the fall of 1959, he began thinking about buying his first car. He had already saved some money from his part-time job at Redpath Pharmacy on the northwest corner of Redpath and Eglinton (later replaced by the first Golden Griddle restaurant, which is still there). Mike made deliveries on his bicycle and worked behind the counter. Phil Lewis, the pharmacist, thought Mike would pursue a career in pharmacy — but that was not to be.

Mike also had a summer job with Ontario Hydro, where his dad worked. A co-worker sold Mike a 1949 Morris Minor for $50 ("I'll never forget the smell of oil and burnt wiring," recalls Mike). It was a two-door with mechanical brakes, just like his dad's 1928 Pontiac, and the headlights were part of the grille surround.

It was grey when he bought it, but Mike has been fond of green cars for as long as he can remember, so he bought a brush and a can of green paint at Canadian Tire and proceeded to paint the car from front to back right at home. He ran out of paint before he got to the back end — but because he had laid it on a bit thick at the front, he pushed the paint with his brush to the rear of the car till all of it was green except for a lip at the lower rear of the body.

The blower for the heater was under the front passenger seat — the car had bucket seats in the front — and Mike could always get a rise out of his passenger by turning on the blower with no warning.

One day, a wheel fell off the Morris right at home and rolled down to the end of their street. Mike's dad saw it rolling but didn't realize at first that it had come from his son's car. The front bumper kept coming out of its socket, and Mike had to keep pushing it back in.

Mike took a year off after high school and worked the night shift for Northern Electric in Stouffville, then enrolled in Chemical Technology at Ryerson in September 1962. He chose Ryerson because a friend decided to go there, and he had a car (a TR-3). No need to wait for the bus. By this time the Morris was gone and Mike was driving a 1958 Hillman Minx four-door sedan purchased from Wietzes Motors on the northeast corner of Mount Pleasant and Broadway, just around the corner from where he lived.

The Hillman was green and white, and Mike sprayed the hubcaps gold to add some extra sparkle. One of these hubcaps flew off into a field somewhere in Scarborough — and Mike left it there, thinking someone would pick it up and believe they had found a lump of gold. All the gauges were in the middle of the dash, and the column shift pattern was reversed. Some teeth were missing from the ring gear, and Mike often had to rock the car back and forth in gear before it would start.

Mike is equally proud of his stainless nail guard, which protects his gas flap and rear fender from nicks and scratches whenever he fills his 13.3-gallon tank.

Fender skirts are normally mounted in the rear wheel openings, but they are not always easy to remove in case of a flat tire. Mike often carries his in the trunk.

Whenever he checks the oil and the rad, Mike uses a broom handle to hoist the hood high up and out of the way. Before he thought of the broom handle, he banged his head eight times on the hood latch. Says Mike, "That locking mechanism is a cranium crusher."

Wietzes Motors, where Mike bought the Hillman, was a Supertest gas station and Rootes dealer selling Sunbeams, Rovers, and Humbers. Mike frequently pumped gas there for extra spending money, and he was fixing a flat on his Hillman when he heard that President Kennedy had been shot.

Now let's fast-forward through the next thirty-plus years, when Mike bought mostly Ford products, most of them green. All the cars he bought from 1965 onward were new cars. He figured that old cars (such as his Morris Minor and Hillman Minx) were nothing but an endless source of trouble.

But his loving wife, Yarmila, knew that Mike still yearned for the car he had fallen in love with as a teenager — a turquoise and white 1955 Pontiac Laurentian two-door hardtop. She wanted to find one and surprise him with it in time for his fiftieth birthday on October 11, 1991. Unfortunately, that particular model was rare and very difficult to find.

Finally, Yarmila enlisted the help of Dean Renwick in searching for Mike's dream car. Dean is well known in the old car hobby and is president of Antique and Classic Auto Appraisal Service. Dean finally located a rare Canadian-built 1955 Pontiac Laurentian two-door hardtop in mint condition, and in the colours Mike wanted.

In June 1996, Dean drove the Pontiac down from Wasaga Beach and parked it in the Fileys' driveway. Mike still didn't know anything about it and was busy inside the house serving refreshments to friends who just happened to drop by. Mike was puzzled to see more and more people drop in, because there seemed to be no particular reason why it should be "open house" at the Fileys.

Then Yarmila called him to the front door. Mike picked up a bag of garbage on the way (the garbage bin was in the garage) and stepped out onto the front porch, where Yarmila was standing. Suddenly he stopped in his tracks when he saw a turquoise and white 1955 Pontiac two-door hardtop parked in their driveway.

Not realizing it was his, he felt slightly annoyed that someone had taken the liberty of parking in their driveway without permission. Then Dean Renwick climbed out from behind the wheel, grinning from ear to ear.

Then Yarmila, followed by a houseful of guests, handed Mike the keys. He couldn't believe it. *This can't be happening to me*, thought Mike, as he slowly approached the car of his dreams — the car he had dreamed of owning for over forty years. *This must be a practical joke. An April Fool's joke in June. This car can't possibly be mine.*

He slid behind the wheel, at Yarmila's urging, and went for a short spin all by himself in his flashy 1955 Pontiac. He drove down Bayview Avenue to the home of friend Paul Godfrey, Mike's publisher at the *Toronto Sun*, where Mike's column has appeared for years. Paul wasn't home, so Mike circled back and pulled into his driveway, greeted by the applause of all their friends still standing on the front lawn.

The truth began to sink in. "This car is mine — all mine," said Mike, giving Yarmila a big, warm hug and kiss.

Mike Filey's Pontiac currently carries the following options: radio, fender skirts (stashed in trunk), outside mirror on driver's side, and heater.

His first big run with his dream car took him down to Lakeshore Boulevard to celebrate the opening of a new TTC streetcar loop near the CNE grounds in late June 1996. Mike was very pleased to have his Pontiac photographed with a beautifully restored 1923 Peter Witt streetcar. Each vehicle evokes an era rich in memories for those who remember when they were new.

That photo appeared in Mike Filey's weekly column, "The Way We Were," in the *Toronto Sun* on Sunday, July 7, 1996. Entitled "Crazy about my automobile," that column announced to Mike's readers that he now owned and was driving a piece of automotive history.

CHAPTER SEVENTEEN:

RON MORASH REMEMBERS HIS FIRST TWO CARS *By Ron Morash*

On April 1, 2004, Ron Morash of St. Albert, Alberta, wrote the following letter to the Old Car Detective.

Dear Bill,

Just recently picked up your great book *60 Years Behind the Wheel* and wanted to let you know what a treasure it is to read and rekindle old memories of the cars we drove in Canada 1900–1960. On page 214 you requested old photos for your next book, along with any background information.

Here is the story behind my first car. The year was 1959, I was fifteen years old and very into cars since purchasing my first car magazines in 1957. Do you remember the pocket-sized *Car Craft* and *Rod & Custom*? Terrific little books and only twenty-five cents.

The car in question was a 1936 Chevrolet Standard five-window coupe with Chevy's inline six cylinder and three-speed floor shift, rear-mounted spare tire, artillery-styled wheels, and turret [metal] roof. We had moved to Penticton, British Columbia, that summer, and I had just sold my three-speed customized bicycle for $50. My uncle Ken Morash had painted the bike 1956 T-Bird turquoise. He worked at Calgary Motor Products Paint & Body Shop, located beside the Bow River, now the mall and promenade to Princess Island Park.

On my way to hockey practice one morning at the Penticton Arena (home of the Penticton Vees — World Hockey Champs, 1953–55), I spotted this terrific looking coupe down a lane. On closer inspection it was for sale and for only $75.

With a little persuasion on my dad, we took it for a test drive, and he was impressed. It helped that he was also a car nut. We bought it on the spot for $65 and drove it home to Kensington Road, where the accompanying photos were taken in our backyard. My new buddies at the time were Rod Cousins, Kenny Almond, and Jimmy Hall (seen here with me and my second car, a 1946 Plymouth two-door with grey primer on the front end).

None of us had our driver's licence, so the 1936 coupe became the vehicle in which we all learned to drive. First it was up and down the lane, about a hundred times a night, then it expanded to two and then three lanes. But that quickly began to tire, so we expanded our trips up the back road behind our street to the dam and turn about at the ranch beside it for the return trip home. All four of us would take turns learning to drive, and being a coupe, only three at a time. It served us well, and all four of us then got our driver's licences.

The cars we took our driver's tests in were as follows: Rod in his dad's 1938 Oldsmobile two-door, Kenny in his dad's 1948 Chevrolet Fleetline two-door, Jimmy in his dad's 1954 Chevrolet Bel Air four-door, and I took my test in Dad's 1959 Chevrolet Bel Air four-door. Can you imagine learning to park in that monster? With the Bat Wings, you could barely see the parking meter out the rear window and mirrors.

One week after getting my driver's licence in March 1960, Rod and I were taking a spin in the 1936 coupe up Campbell's Mountain. It was the mountain with "Penticton" written on it in whitewash stones about eight feet high. We had driven up to the lookout and were returning, perhaps a little too fast, around a hairpin turn near the bottom on loose gravel.

We spun out, did a 180-degree turn, hitting the side bank, flipping over a barbed wire fence, landing on our roof on a rock the same size as the turret top,

Four buddies in Penticton, British Columbia, in 1961 with Ron's 1946 Plymouth two-door sedan. (Left to right) Rod Cousins, Kenny Almond, Jimmy Hall, Ron Morash.

then bounced back on our wheels. Rod and I must have blanked out temporarily as we awoke in a heap, asking each other if we were okay, then realized what had happened, both in a daze with steam streaming from the radiator. We walked the rest of the way down to Rod's grandparents' orchard on Upper Bench Road and telephoned his dad. My dad was out of town. He was a travelling salesman for Pauline's Cookies. [Author's note: Remember Pauline's Cream Puffs — chocolate-coated marshmallows with cherry-flavoured centres.]

Ron's dark blue 1936 Chevrolet five-window coupe, looking toward southwest Penticton and Lake Skaha.

Mr. Cousins, always calm and collected, phoned the auto wreckers and came to our rescue with the tow truck, a 1947 Ford one-ton. Later that week when my dad came home, I handed him my driver's licence, and he said, "What's this for?" I told him what had happened and he gave it back to me and said, "When you fall off, get back on the horse."

We pushed the roof out with our feet, lying on our backs on the seat. I drove that Chevy until August 1960 and sold it to a friend of Rod's for $65. He then drove it home to Kamloops and promptly chopped the roof off. I then bought my 1946 Plymouth for $90, then sold it in 1961 for $125. and moved back to Calgary.

Unfortunately, Rod Cousins drowned in a boating accident in November 1963, the same month as President Kennedy's assassination. Other great cars followed, but none bring back the great memories of our 1936 Chevrolet coupe.

In 1975, Ron and Barbara Morash purchased a 1935 Chrevrolet four-door for $700, then restored it over the next eight years. "What goes around comes around. We had paid back to history for the damage we did to the 1936 coupe. We kept the 1935 for twenty years and donated it to the Reynolds Alberta Museum in Wetaskawin, Alberta, in 1995."

Ron's 1936 coupe with spare tire and artillery wheels, looking toward northeast Penticton with Campbell Mountain in background.

CHAPTER EIGHTEEN

DR. BOB McGIRR REMEMBERS MATILDA

On Thursday, January 8, 2004, Dr. Bob McGirr and I headed out of town in his car for the monthly executive meeting of the Leamington-Mersea Historical Society. I brought along my little pocket-sized tape recorder to capture Bob's recollections of an old car named Matilda in case we had a spare few minutes during the meeting.

At first, it didn't work out that way. We all talked non-stop till finally our president, Bob McCracken, declared the meeting adjourned at 3:30 p.m. We then all hopped into our respective vehicles to head for home. Bob and I climbed into his car just as the last other car drove away. Dr. Bob turned the key to start his car. Nothing. The battery was dead. Back into the museum to call for a tow truck on Bob's CAA Plus card. We were told we might have to wait a while before help arrived.

What great luck! After Bob made his call, I turned on the tape recorder in the museum basement and captured the story you are now about to read. One question from me was all that Bob needed to swing into action: "Dr. Bob, when did Matilda first come into your life?"

Bob McMillan is simonizing Matilda's hood. The lady in the photo is his mother. This picture was taken by Rev. McMillan (Bob's father) in the backyard of the manse of Wentworth United Church in Hamilton, where he served as pastor. It is possible that Matilda was given to him by one of his parishioners.

"Well, I first met Matilda in the fall of 1949. She was a 1928 Pontiac car, two seater and a rumble seat. She was in excellent condition."

"What colour was she?"

"She was a pale mid-green; the tires were in excellent condition, I'm sure they must have been replaced many times. She was bought from a junkyard in Hamilton and was owned by Reverend McMillan, and his son was one of our housemates at 255 Willingdon Avenue in Kingston. There were three of us who were living in this house of a widow by the name of Mrs. Graham; she was the widow of a prior mayor, also a very, very highly respected builder. The house was just immaculate. The driveway was scrubbed glistening white, and that does have a bearing on the story."

"Now when would this have been, when you were there?"

"We started medicine at Queen's, and it was a six-year course. It ran from 1948 to 1954. However, in the first year we were on our own, on shank's mare. So it would be September 1949, when we were entering our second year, when Bob McMillan drove down in Matilda at an average speed of about twenty-two miles an hour from Hamilton. I think it took him about ten hours."

"And he or his dad had found the car in a junkyard?"

"Yes. Found it in a junkyard. They had done a few little minor repairs, and the original colour was there. Everything was original.

"Wow! Now, did it have wooden spoke wheels or steel spoke wheels?"

"My recollection is that it had dark brownish-yellow wooden spokes, which were loose! I told Bob about the trick of driving it into the nearest creek [to get the spokes to swell up and tighten], and he told me he was reserving a spot for me in the psychiatric ward of Kingston General. So I said, well, that may be, but if you want to try it out, it works.

"The wintertime was very difficult on Matilda. She only made about nine miles to the gallon with a strong wind blowing at the back. Kingston was fairly level in the outer parts, but we lived in Kingston proper, and about a

Ron McAuley (one of the "Three Musty Steers") is leaning against Matilda in this early 1950s photo in Kingston. He's wearing the Queen's Medical School jacket designed by Bob McGirr.

block away was the penitentiary. People never admitted there was a penitentiary inside Kingston. It was one block outside.

"We used Matilda for the purpose of getting to class. Now on a cold day we'd take a little 'borrowed' can (which meant we filched it) of ether from the chemistry lab, so we gave her a shot of ether. The bonnet, or hood, had side flaps, so we took both flaps up, gave her a shot of ether, then we took two teaspoons of raw gasoline and fed it down through the butterfly valve of the carburetor, quickly put the one side flap down, then I threw a match in and ran. And, of course, the explosion was substantial. Then she would start to chug — *chugga-chugga-chugga* — and the vibration would just about throw you out of the car.

"Finally, when she warmed up, she was just beautiful. She purred. And then into town we went with the three of us squeezed into the front seat. On a cold day it might be five degrees below zero."

"And the car would have a floorshift?"

"Yes, all tightly compressed. And I recall the windshield had little adjusting arms and knobs on the side, so in the summertime it could be sloped and opened. Someone had added side mirrors somewhere along the way, and it had a kind of velveteen interior, dark blue with little elastic pockets on the side. And inside one of them we found a manual, which came in handy when we broke an axle. I had never actually done one myself, but when I was about ten years old in Winnipeg [around 1932], one of our neighbours had a Moon, and he had replaced an axle in his backyard. In order to keep the dirt out, he had put it on big sheets of cardboard. So the three of us replaced the broken axle in Matilda. It cost us three dollars at the local junkyard. He thought we were insane. Our landlady, Mrs. Emma Graham, happened to be away for a week, and her daughter was in charge. And her daughter had many misgivings. She said, 'Don't you dare get a spot of oil on my mother's driveway.'"

"That would be grounds for eviction."

"That's right. The garage was empty in this beautifully built house, and they allowed us to park Matilda inside during the winter, but we always pushed her outside before applying the ether and gasoline."

"You didn't want the garage to burn down."

"No. She was very difficult to drive in the freezing rain. The wheels tended to get caught in the ruts, and Princess Street had about a forty-degree decline. It was like going down a ski hill without poles."

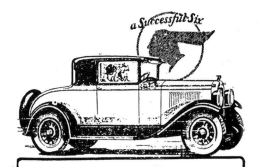

Leamington Post & News, May 17, 1928. This was the first year that Pontiac had four-wheel brakes.

"Was there a red triangle on one of the rear fenders for four-wheel brakes?"

"Yes, there was, and there was also a little round silver thing to step on — you were never to put your foot on the fender."

"Ah. For getting up into the rumble seat."

"Yes. Bess and I had our first date, and we sat in the rumble seat, and Bob McMillan and his girlfriend Lorraine sat in the front. [Bess remembers it differently: "The other couple sat in the rumble seat while Bob and I rode inside." Now back to Bob's version.] Then it began to rain, and we had brought an umbrella. This would be in October. We drove down to the Strand along the waterfront and looked at the moon on the water."

"Did the back window go up and down so the two couples could communicate?"

"That I don't ever recall, I don't think it did, but it had a curtain, a silken curtain. And when the evening progressed, the little blind inside was discreetly pulled down."

"Of course, you could always knock on the glass."

"That's right. So after we were just about frozen, we knocked on the window, and we all decided — since there was no heater in it, it got a little cool — so back to the house we went."

"What's the proper etiquette when you're out on a date in a rumble seat? Did you climb in first or did Bess?"

"I stepped up onto the running board and then onto the little step on the fender. Then I stood inside. There wasn't much room. Then she got halfway up and I helped her in."

"Leather upholstery?"

"It was the cheapest plastic I had ever seen. Obviously it was not the original. It was all cracked. And Bess was very reticent about sitting on this wretched seat at first, but we found a beautiful big car rug, and we put it down first and then folded it over our feet."

"I understand that Matilda got a fresh coat of paint while at Queen's."

"Over the course of years, we had repainted her in Queen's colours: red, blue, and gold. No longer was it a nondescript mid-green. Now I think the blue was the body colour, and the red and gold in parallel stripes. It was the gaudiest thing you'd ever see."

"Wow!"

"And we painted the tires too. And they started to peel a month after."

"Did you drive Matilda to football games?"

"No, it was a little difficult manoeuvring through the heavy crowds, and the car drew a lot of abuse. People would say, 'Hey, Mac, try second gear!' when we already had it in high. Or 'Have you considered replacing this vehicle?' or 'This is awful. Why don't you donate it to a museum?'"

"And this, of course, was back in the days before people began to appreciate old cars."

"Oh yes. The idea was to get rid of them. Get them off the road and scrap them."

"Now, Matilda would have had a fabric insert on the roof. Did the roof ever leak?"

"Not to my knowledge, but Bob used to paint it about once a month. And he found a can of waterproof glue or something, and he went all around the edges. I think that roof was the original."

"I'll bet it was."

"Now the back seat — in the rumble seat — was not. The floorboards were interesting because I think they were the resurrected, recycled hardwood boards from the Globe-a-Lite Battery Company."

"Wow! And so Bob McMillan was the owner of the car. I wonder what he paid for it."

"It was under fifty. And I don't think he got a nickel for it when it was scrapped."

"And how long was Matilda on the road?"

"This went on through 1949, 1950, 1951, 1952 and then toward our last year at Queen's, it disappeared."

"The car?"

"The car. Apparently Bob's sister (I've forgotten her name now) was a schoolteacher living in Hamilton and teaching in one of the surrounding communities. She was driving back and forth to summer school in Matilda, and it conked out on top of Hamilton Mountain. Someone said, 'Why don't you put it in neutral and let it roll down the side of the mountain?' And she said, 'Not on your life, boy!' Even though her home was right at the base of the mountain at Wentworth United Church. She took a streetcar home and left Matilda on the mountain. She came back a few days later with a tow truck and Matilda was hauled away to the junkyard. And nothing further was ever heard of Matilda."

"Maybe it went back to the same junkyard it was rescued from five years earlier."

"I think it did."

Dr. Bob tells me the weather was cold up on the mountain, and Matilda's battery may have given up the ghost. And before the end of their 1952–53 year at Queen's, Bob McMillan told his other two pals that Matilda had "gone west." I asked Bob, "So did you fellows have another car during your final year at Queen's?"

"No. We walked. We found that six hours of lectures every day was a lot and we needed to walk it off."

"And there were still the three of you…"

"Yes. Bob McMillan and Ron Mcauley were both from Hamilton, and all three of us started meds at Queen's in the fall of 1948. We were the class of 1954."

"And all three of you went through together."

"All went through together. They called us the Three Musty Steers, after the Three Musketeers."

"And did you all graduate together?"

"We all graduated."

"And where did the other two fellows go?

"Well, Bob went to Hamilton, and I think he interned at the Hamilton General. And Ron McAuley went to St. Louis, Missouri, into internal medicine, and then the following year he came back to get his Senior at Kingston. And I went to the University of Western Ontario and interned at the old Victoria Hospital, right beside the Thames River."

From there, Dr. Bob went to the Hospital for Sick Children in Toronto from July 1955 to July 1956. And now, with all his training completed, he decided it was time to buy his first car. He recalled, "We bought the car around March of 1956 — a 1956 Dodge — and it had the first fins. It was a four-door and a very, very bright canary blue."

It also had whitewall tires. Bob purchased the car from Elgin Motors in downtown Toronto. The salesman's name was Mr. Rogers (not the TV star). This was the car that brought Dr. Bob and his wife, Bess, to Leamington when they moved here in 1956.

Among their luggage and belongings was Dr. Bob's red, gold, and blue Queen's Medical School leather jacket — the same colours painted on Matilda when she was still being driven in Kingston. I asked, "Dr. Bob, do you still have your Queen's leather jacket?" He said, "No."

It turns out that Dr. Bob had to make a house call to someone on the tenth concession north of town soon after he and Bess moved to Leamington. The weather that night was wretched, and after administering medical attention to the person in need, Dr. Bob discovered the rear wheels of his 1956 Dodge were stuck in a rut on the gravel road. Rocking the car back and forth didn't help. Finally, he looked in the trunk for something to put under one of the rear wheels.

The only thing he could find was his red, gold, and blue Queen's leather jacket. Down into the rut it went, hard side up against one of the rear wheels. Then back into the car, where Dr. Bob's foot rammed the gas pedal to the floor. His canary blue 1956 Dodge shot forward out of the rut while his Queen's Medical School leather jacket sailed through the air in the opposite direction. And that's the last he saw of it. If his car was facing east, we could say that his jacket, like Matilda, has "gone west."

CHAPTER NINETEEN:

OVIDE PAZZY'S 1951 CHEVROLET *By Robert Pazzy*

On March 8, 2004, Robert Pazzy of St-Marc-Sur-Richelieu, Quebec, wrote the following letter to the Old Car Detective.

Dear Bill Sherk,

Following your request for cars for your next book after *60 Years Behind the Wheel*, it is with pleasure that I send you a picture of my father's car. This car was bought used in 1955 at Chevrolet Motors Sales in downtown Montreal where my father used to work as a mechanic.

The car is a dark grey 1951 Chevrolet. This photo was taken by my mother, Jeannette Beland, on September 18, 1955, during our first trip to Plattsburgh, New York. My father, Ovide, is pictured in front of the car with sister Liliane in his arms. If you look closely, you can see my brother Frank at the wheel. He was seven years old at the time.

Looking forward to reading your next book. I really enjoyed *60 Years Behind the Wheel.*

CHAPTER TWENTY:

MY FIRST MERCURY FLATHEAD (1968 – 1975) By Vern Kipp

This 1953 Mercury Monterey four-door sedan in a magazine ad is identical to the car owned by Vern Kipp so many years ago — identical except for the driver, seen here with a fedora (Vern doesn't wear one).

The story of this car began in the pages of the *Toronto Star* in March 1968. Always an avid reader of the want ads and looking for old autos, I noticed an ad describing a 1953 Mercury Monterey sedan.

The best part of the ad indicated an asking price of only $150. A call confirmed a running, complete auto ready to drive away. An old vacant lot on Pape Avenue just south of the railway tracks and just north of Gerrard on the west side was the location. The lot was "paved" with crushed cinders, and a fairly big man with a cigar clamped in his mouth greeted me. He reminded me of an old carnival huckster, but I quickly decided the old Merc was just what my car-crazed mind needed.

I have always loved the big, long mufflers on the old flathead-powered Mercs, and this one had just the sound I enjoyed.

Noticing the right front window was missing, I quickly indicated a "no sale" if it wasn't replaced. He said, "No problem. I have a 1963 Rambler being parted out over there in the corner." With that, he indicated the Rambler with a sweep of his big hand.

"Baloney," I said, "There's no way it will fit."

"Oh, yes it will," he said, as he asked me for a deposit in the next breath.

I protested at first until he reminded me his name was Norm Charlton, and [he was] "famous for good deals." Just by coincidence I had heard of his reputation through the grapevine just days before and the vibes were good ones. Also, he wore an old fedora hat, and hats were fast disappearing on men's heads. This guy was a holdover from the old days.

The following day after work I took delivery of my "new" old car, and, yes, the window fit just as he said it would. No mechanical fitness was required, and so I drove the car home and garaged it behind the house. My daily driver, a 1953 Meteor Mainline, was now relegated to the street in front of the house.

Just days later, attempts to start the car indicated a dead battery. A trip to my nearby BA station at Patricia and Danforth indicated it was badly discharged. Two dollars later it was up, and so were my spirits, only to have this repeat itself over and over. My next solution was to buy a battery charger from Canadian Tire (I still have it!). The battery, it turned out, was good, but I had what I later learned was a dead short, and the only solution was to disconnect the battery.

A request to troubleshoot the wiring at the BA station indicated they didn't touch this aspect of car repair, and they recommended one Fred Brittain on the next street in an old red brick garage. He was so busy he couldn't come by for a month, but no matter. The Merc was a collector car and a keeper. I felt like I had a trophy, and just garaging it made me feel good.

Finally he came by and she ran again (after he sorted out the bird's nest that had been the main wiring harness). That summer that car was used sparingly because when warm it always gave me trouble. By September, though, it started better, much better.

Then another 1953 Merc came to light! Spotted by my brother on Danforth Road just northeast of the Scarborough House Hotel was an identical four-door sedan, and bottle green as well. Closer examination revealed it to be a custom model with a standard transmission (my 1953 was an automatic).

Nearby were three dump trucks, and inside the car, large cans of oil and gas on the back seat. In those days the owner's name was required on all trucks, so on a hunch I called the number on the truck. As I suspected, that was the owner, and because the block was cracked, the car was now a storage shed!

He was willing to sell the car for $30, no less, because it had a perfect hood, trunk lid, bumpers, doors, and best of all a perfect steering wheel. I had to have this car for parts. A $10 tow home brought my investment up to $40. Once home, a new home had to be found for my "good" 1953 Merc.

Because the bottom of our backyard jutted into the lane out back, it wasn't possible to parallel park across my garage doors and yard. With tape in my hand I discovered I could squeeze the parts car in if I straightened the fence out. Our yard was only 16 feet wide but 120 feet deep. Determination made it happen, and I set to work wrecking my first ever parts car. I was able to remove the doors of this car inside the garage, and in short order all my desired parts were removed.

When I called my local wrecker, Cliff Jones at Victoria Park and Danforth, I was asked if the car had a rad. Because prices for scrap were so low the radiator would make it worth their while to come out. Reluctantly, I gave them the rad, and the "old scow" was taken for scrap.

Immediately I changed both right doors on my "good" Merc, and new pride began to take over. Next the hood ornament was changed, and finally the steering wheel, with Fred Brittain's help. Then I set to work sanding down the body and priming it with grey primer. Driving it to work gave me a new pride of ownership as well. But it did stand out, and not in a good way.

The cream top, orange primered quarters, a grey primed hood and fenders, and bottle green doors stressed a motorcycle cop to the point of pulling me over at Brimley Road and Sheppard in mid-summer. He was convinced I had a junker, and he started pounding the floors with his motorcycle boots.

Just then a co-worker on his way home pulled in behind my car. Davey Warren was the guy's name, and he was furious with the cop. "Don't you recognize this guy's trying to restore this car!" he said. "What's wrong with you anyway?" He then gave him a sermon about speeders, and the cop vanished.

Repeating this at home brought a new description of the 1953 from my mother: "Joseph's coat" she called the car, and the name stuck. I realized then it was like a patch-work quilt and I would have to paint it ASAP or risk further police fury.

The following year I discovered vintage trucks and bought two in short order. Now owning a retreat property and renting two garages and two parking spaces close to home created a car-buying frenzy of a sort, and yet, looking back, it was a unique time. For $200 I bought a 1952 Merc half-ton pickup, for $100 a 1951 Merc coupe. Collectors were few, and cars were plentiful.

Between September 1970 and July 1974, at least twenty vehicles were picked up, stored, traded, scrapped, etc. The 1953 Merc joined the 1952 Merc half-ton, and a 1937

Oldsmobile coupe at the retreat property and became "the northern collection." Only one was barn stored and the Mercs slowly rusted outside.

Starting them up and moving them around kept them limber and the 1953 was rotated just once. I nicknamed her "the Northern Queen." Obviously a solution would be to build a building or modify an old barn to accept more than one car, but this was not to be.

The spring of 1975 was unusually warm and dry, and on May 10 I made a later than usual trip to the property to open up the old house (built in 1920) and take stock. The car I drove up there was a 1950 Mercury coupe (I still own it!) purchased in July 1973. On arrival I went down the hill to draw a pail of water, but unknown to me, a relative started a fire in the stove in the living room with the dampers left open.

Then while that person wandered outside, my worst fears were suddenly realized. A flaming bird's nest built in an upper chimney on the second floor was blown into the grass behind the house. Normally the grass is green on May 10, but this year there had been nineteen straight days with no rain whatsoever. A strong southwest wind blew and humidity was only 27 percent that day. I had cautioned my relative that checking the dampers was a necessary precaution, but it was forgotten this one fateful day, and the fire was lit first!

With thirty-three acres clear and sixty-seven acres in trees the fire roared in every direction. I raced out to my neighbours to place an alarm with Lands and Forests (I had no phone), then back again. Convinced the house would survive because of a concrete base around the perimeter, I watched in horror as the fire tunnelled under a storm porch, then went up through the floors, and the house was lost.

Also destroyed in thirty minutes: three vehicles, one two-room cabin, two small barns, and thirty-three acres

Vern is past president of the Early Ford V8 Club of America, Southern Ontario Region, and he loves to visit vintage wrecking yards in search of parts to help fellow members restore their cars. I snapped this photo of Vern in an old auto wreckers east of Toronto just after he liberated a sun visor from the pitiful remains of this 1947-48 Ford coach. Someone had painted the visor turquoise years earlier.

Here we see Vern gently removing the stainless trim from the hood of this 1946 Ford sedan while his junkyard dog, Beth, stands on guard.

of meadow land. By a miracle the bush was still wet and the fire went northeast into the timber. There it was met by my neighbours and a Lands and Forest fire crew. By nightfall it was finally out, smouldering stumps and all. My nearby neighbour lost twenty-two acres of trees.

The 1950 Mercury with front tires on fire was driven out on the sand road, and by a miracle the flames went out. Not only that, the people inside, including myself, were saved from possible smoke inhalation and an untimely end. The Northern Queen (my 1953 Mercury Monterey) glowed cherry red after the gas tank exploded, and it was the end of a fine old car. Just an old four-door, someone could say, but my first project and a lot of memories.

Vern is half inside the trunk of this 1952-54 Ford or Meteor, hoping to rescue from the top of the gas tank the sending unit that operates the gas gauge on the dashboard. The rescue was a success!

Epilogue: The retreat property (in Sabine Township) was sold in September 1981 and some salvage parts removed. One was the heart of the old 1953 Merc, her original replacement engine. That engine now beats in a 1949 Meteor, and that car is still on the road.

CHAPTER TWENTY-ONE

DON BARNES' FIRST CAR

Don Barnes recalls, "My 1947 Chevrolet was purchased by me in 1957, the year of my sixteenth birthday, for $300. It was ten years old, 37,000 miles, and black in colour. Over the next two years I modified it: 1950 Plymouth grille, nosed and decked, frenched 1949 Ford blue-dot tail lights, sixteen-inch Caddy full wheel discs with Olds spinners, two-inch lowering blocks, fender skirts, split manifold, dual exhaust with glasspaks, 1949 Chevy licence plate bracket on the rear, and hooded headlights. The paint was 1956 Chevy Sierra Gold Metallic."

Other details add flash and dash to this vintage auto: whitewall tires, a radio aerial on top of the left front fender, and pinstriping on the leading edge of the hood. Note the Olds spinners on the Caddy wheel discs. Don only needed two instead of four because the rear wheels had fender skirts.

Like thousands of other young fellows back then, Don must have been an avid reader of the many little hot rod and custom car magazines so popular in the late 1950s. And only twenty-five cents. There was *Rod and Custom, Rodding and Restying, Car Craft, Car Speed and Style*, and others. Don's cool Chevy would look right at home in the pages of any of them.

"This photo was taken just outside Parkhill, Ontario, on one of our farms. In 1964 I left Parkhill to take a job at American Motors of Canada in Brampton, which was then taken over by Renault, then taken over by Chrysler, and then taken over by Daimler. I have retired, as of January 2000, and now reside in St. Thomas, Ontario. I enjoyed your first book, *60 Years Behind the Wheel*."

CHAPTER TWENTY-TWO

DEWANE TETZLAFF'S COOL METEOR AND RED-HOT PLYMOUTH FURY

This gleaming black 1959 Plymouth Fury was Dewane Tetzlaff's first new car. With its 318-cubic-inch V8, it was one of the hottest cars in Leamington at that time. This photo was taken in the family driveway at 50 Fox Street when the car was new. That's Dewane behind the wheel.

Dewane Tetzlaff was born on Tuesday, September 18, 1934, in a white frame farmhouse still standing on the fifth concession north of Leamington, Ontario, and two miles east of the home where Dewane and his wife, Peggy, have lived for nearly forty years.

The family moved into town, and Dewane grew up in the Tetzlaff home at 50 Fox Street. It was heated with a coal furnace. A relative down the street had a garage a car and a half wide, and here is where the Tetzlaffs stored their coal, alongside their relatives' car. It was Dewane's responsibility to bring the coal on his wagon along the sidewalk from that garage to their house. He had the key to the garage, and the car key was attached to it. And when no one was looking, he started up the car and drove it back and forth in the driveway.

Dewane earned his spending money by delivering the *Windsor Star* to 220 customers. He also worked part-time at Irv Cantor's IGA store and later at Dave Korneilson's BA station, where Oak Street meets Highway 3.

He bought his first car around 1953, a two-tone green 1949 Mercury four-door sedan with whitewalls and a radio. The previous owner was Harold Gray, a neighbour on Fox Street. Gray worked at the Ford plant in Windsor and drove back and forth every day. The car was still in excellent shape with over 100,000 miles on it when Dewane bought it for about $350.

His next car was a 1954 Meteor Victoria two-door hardtop. It was all stock when he bought it off Paul Wigle's used car lot on Highway 77 just north of Leamington. One day in winter, when the roads were slippery, he was driving past the Metropolitan Hospital in Windsor and hit the brakes to stop for a red light. He slid on ice into the intersection and hit another car.

No one was injured, but the front end of the Meteor was smashed in, and it couldn't be driven away. Dewane returned to Windsor with a cousin from Blytheswood, and they towed the Meteor to his parents' house at 50 Fox Street, where Dewane was still living.

The car sat on the street for a couple of days while Dewane pondered his next move. He then took the car to Lloyd Thomas, a body man in nearby Wheatley. He told Lloyd he wanted a different grille, different tail lights, a shaved trunk lid, and a cable under the dash to pop the trunk open.

When it was finished, the Meteor had a 1954 Chevy grille, Olds 98 tail lights, 1956 Dodge Royal Lancer wheel covers, Hollywood mufflers, and a lowered rear end with bubble skirts from Rossini's hot rod shop in nearby Chatham. Dewane drove with the skirts off in the winter and padlocked on in the summer.

Sometime during 1959, he met a fellow from Merlin at a dance in Comber. The Meteor was parked outside — and the man from Merlin just had to have it. He made Dewane an offer he couldn't refuse, and the Meteor was gone.

By this time Dewane was working at the Chrysler plant in Windsor, and he decided

Dewane Tetzlaff was the proud owner of this two-tone customized 1954 Meteor two-door hardtop in the late 1950s, when he was a member of the Leamington Road Runners Rod and Custom Club. He has carried this photo in his wallet for over forty years.

Dewane's wife, Peggy, was photographed next to her dad's 1951 Chevrolet in the late 1950s, when polka-dot dresses were the latest fashion. She still has the dress.

it was time to buy a new car. He went to Hyatt Motors, the Plymouth-Chrysler dealership in Leamington, and ordered a black 1959 Plymouth Fury two-door hardtop with the 318 V8 with a four-barrel carb, three-speed Torque-Flite transmission, crash pad, deluxe steering wheel, radio with rear seat speakers, and 8:25 whitewall tires.

Because he worked in production control at Chrysler, Dewane was able to follow his new car right through the factory as it was being manufactured — and he was the one who drove it off the end of the assembly line. How many other car owners have done that?

This 1959 Fury was part of Dewane's life for many years. He and Peggy were married in the Leamington United Church in 1960, and they were still driving that car after the birth of their three sons, Alan, Dale, and Doug. Those little fellows loved climbing onto the roof in the wintertime and sliding down onto the hood while the car was parked in their driveway.

By the early 1970s, Dewane had driven the Fury at least 150,000 miles. By this time, the bottom of the rear fenders had rotted out. To restore the car's appearance he put heavy plastic bags inside the fenders and poured cement into the bags. Because the fenders were tapered downward, the cement filled up the rotted area and stayed in place. He then sprayed the plastic bags black to match the rest of the car.

Eventually rust took its toll, and the Fury sat in the driveway while the family moved on to a 1975 Chevy and other more contemporary vehicles. Finally the Fury was towed to a local wrecking yard — a one-owner car to the very end.

CHAPTER TWENTY-THREE

THE BALZER-PICKFORD MODEL A COUPE

Henry Ford built over four million Model A Fords from 1928 to 1931. This is the story of one of them, long after it left the factory and showroom.

Bill Balzer and a friend purchased a 1931 Model A Ford coupe from a farmer near Schomberg, Ontario, in the late 1950s for $25 (they each kicked in $12.50, then Bill later bought out his friend). It wasn't running, and the fabric insert roof was rotten, but the car itself was solid — and perfect for building up into a hot rod.

Bill and his friend towed it home behind Bill's 1950 Chevy pickup truck, using a Mercury outboard motor start cord. The Model A had no brakes, so whenever Bill slowed down, it banged into the back of his truck. They were just passing the Six Points in the west end of Toronto when the cord broke. The Model A rolled on ahead, out of control, and began passing Bill on the right. His friend by now was standing straight up with his head through the fabric roof, yelling "No brakes!" Then the car rolled into a ditch.

Ron Pickford stands proudly beside the chopped Model A coupe he purchased from Bill Balzer. Note the deuce grille shell and the low stance of the roof, which made it difficult for Ron to see the overhead traffic lights whenever he drove the car to Buffalo. This photo was taken in 1959 in the west end of Toronto.

With the Model A finally home in one piece, Bill began to rebuild it. He owned a 1941 Merc coupe at the time, which he scrapped, then put the Merc dashboard in the Model A and welded the Merc roof to the roof of the Model A to cover up the rotted insert. Bill found it fit really well — then he smoothed it off till you'd swear it came that way from the factory.

This side view of the Balzer-Pickford Model A shows the flame painting leaping from the top of the hood and the nerf bar out back. It's a cool, wicked, lean, mean, black-primered bundle of tire-squealing horsepower.

He replaced the old four-banger with a 1941 Ford flathead V8 taken from a 1937 Ford that had been T-boned (hit from the side). Eager for extra horsepower, Bill replaced the single-carb manifold with a dual carb setup. When he finished, he had more tools than when he started because he found a screwdriver lying in the valley of the block when he removed the single-carb manifold.

You want to be able to drive your hot rod fast without overheating. Bill solved this problem by installing aluminum heads from a Canadian truck engine. These were thicker and provided better cooling.

When Bill chopped the top, he kept cutting down and down till it looked right. It was chopped a full five inches. Then Bill installed a front leather seat from a Hillman because it was the only seat flat enough to fit. Whenever Bill went over a bump, his head hit the inside of the roof.

To pick up the rock-'n'roll tunes being blasted out by CHUM Radio, Bill installed a radio from a Nash Metropolitan on the rear window shelf. Also, he cut off the bottom of the cowl-mounted gas tank and installed a Cadillac gas tank, which he jumped on to flatten enough to fit.

As a finishing touch, he installed a set of gauges on the ceiling just above the windshield — making the interior of the Model A resemble the cockpit of an airplane.

This feature may have prompted Ron Pickford to purchase the coupe from Bill Balzer by 1959. Ron worked for Air Canada at the time (he now sells cars for Courtesy Chev-Olds-Cadillac after thirty-four years with Air Canada).

Ron drove the car a lot (as Bill had done) and decided it needed a heater for cold weather driving. There was no room to fit one under the dash, so Ron finally got a heater from a 1947 Cadillac hearse and mounted it right behind the seat.

One day, Ron and a friend, Bob Canning, headed for Cloverdale Mall, alongside Highway 427, where the British Empire Motor Club was organizing a car rally. Ron's chopped A coupe (by now flame-painted) looked strangely out of place amid all the Jaguars and MGAs, but sign up they did, and they headed off into the countryside with a sheet of instructions, Ron driving and Bob navigating.

Bob had an uncanny sense for calculating the right time and distance from checkpoint to checkpoint. They were right on the money every step of the way till they made a wrong turn near Terra Cotta. They wandered two miles off course before they realized their mistake. Pouring on the gas, they raced along a gravel road till they were back on track. They came in a close second that day and took home a big trophy.

Ron finally decided to sell his hot little coupe. He put an ad in the paper and a fellow from up north bought it and took it home. He said he was going to put a Hemi in it. Maybe he did.

In the spring of 1997, I enjoyed an interesting visit with Bill Balzer (left) at a swap meet in Waterdown, Ontario, where he supplied many details for this story. I'm holding a photo he gave me of a chopped 1934 Ford three-window coupe from years ago. Another story for another book.

CHAPTER TWENTY-FOUR:

BILL MYERS REMEMBERS A 1936 CHEVROLET

Bill Myers of Pickering, Ontario, will never forget his first car. It was 1954 and he was seventeen when he kicked in about $10 with three of his pals to buy a 1936 Chevy two-door sedan for $50 from the back row of Ted Davey's used car lot on Danforth Avenue in the east end of Toronto.

It had a bullet hole in the trunk lid, but the salesman didn't explain how it got there. He was just happy to take their money. They drove away along the Danforth, filled with pride of ownership. They each owned a piece of this car.

At the first stoplight, they discovered the shocks were shot. The car bounced up and down for the entire time they waited for the light to turn green.

Soon after that, the starter died — not a problem when the car has four owners. With one fellow behind the wheel, the other three pushed it up to about 10 miles per hour in second gear — then popped the clutch and the car was running! The three fellows pushing then jumped up on the running boards and climbed in through the windows as the car roared off down the street.

Then the day rolled around when they decided to rebuild the engine. There was nothing wrong with the engine (the car was running fine), but they knew that other people rebuilt engines in old cars, so why couldn't they?

And so, out came the engine and down it went into Bill Myers' parents' basement, where the four owners took it all apart, then didn't know how to put it back together. At this realization, they began to lose interest in the project. And so all the engine parts lay scattered in the Myerses' basement.

Finally Bill Myers' dad pulled the plug: "Get this junk out of here." The small pieces went out with the regular garbage, but the engine block was too big and too heavy to fit into the family's garbage can.

Bill and the other three owners heaved it up the basement stairs and into a big wheelbarrow, then down to the edge of the ravine at the end of the street in the upscale and very conservative Beaches district of east-end Toronto. They tipped the wheelbarrow and watched the engine block roll down the hill to the bottom of the ravine. It's probably still there under the mud.

Meanwhile, the engineless 1936 Chevy was still parked in the Myerses' driveway. The boys were told to get rid of it. Not having enough money for a tow truck, they began pushing it along Kingston Road in search of a wrecking yard.

A man pulled up behind them and, thinking they were out of gas, offered to push them to the nearest service station. The boys told him the car had no engine. "That's okay," the man said, "I'll push you anyway."

And so this once proud 1936 Chevrolet was ignominiously pushed along Kingston Road by a fellow motorist who took pity on it. Finally he had to turn off, and the boys were left once again with a car that had no means of propulsion.

Tired at the thought of more pushing, they shoved the old Chevy onto a residential side street, then scattered in all directions, leaving the old car abandoned in the middle of the street.

This ad appeared in the Leamington Post & News on February 6, 1936. The new 1936 Chevrolet illustrated is the four-door sedan. Bill Myers and his three pals bought the two-door model for $50 in 1954.

CHAPTER TWENTY-FIVE:

JERRY SHUSTER REMEMBERS TWO 1936 CHEVROLETS

This maroon 1939 Plymouth four-door sedan with built-in trunk was the Shuster family car when this photo was taken north of Leamington around 1947. Diane (born in 1937) is at the driver's window, Jerry (1939) is behind her, and Milan (1941) is on the running board. Note the snap-on metal whitewalls, a popular substitute for real whitewalls after the war. Note also the fancy ringed bumper guard and the absence of a front licence plate. (Because of wartime metal shortages, no front plates were issued in Ontario from 1943 to 1947.)

Jerry Shuster was born on October 4, 1939, and grew up in Leamington, Ontario. As soon as he turned sixteen, he took his test for his driver's licence, and he passed! He walked out of the licence office beaming with pride. He was now a member of the motoring public. And adding to the excitement, many of his high school buddies were getting their licences around the same time.

Now Jerry began dreaming of buying a car of his own. He had a part-time job at the big new Loblaws store near the centre of town and began saving his money. In June 1958 he graduated from high school in Leamington and landed a summer job with Canada Bread right in town. This gave him the financial security he needed to make the big leap into the adult world: the purchase of his first car. "My first car was a '36 Chev," he recalls. "The owner wanted $50 but I got him down to $25. Then I drove it home."

Jerry drove all around town that summer in his twenty-five-dollar car, his chest swelling with so much pride he could barely turn the steering wheel. Then September rolled around, and he headed off to the University of Toronto for his first year of Engineering. His 1936 Chevy stayed home, patiently awaiting his return next spring.

In the summer of 1959, Jerry got a job with the Leamington Public Utilities Commission (a government job!), and this added sense of financial security prompted him to spend some money on his car. Then, as now, it was helpful if you had a second old car that you could cannibalize for parts to keep the other one on the road. We've all heard of the two-car family; well, in the summer of 1959, Jerry became a two-car teenager.

"I saw another '36 Chev and told the guy, 'I wouldn't mind your car for parts.' We dickered over the price, and he agreed to $25, then 'Sparky' Clark and I went there to pick it up. And when we got there, the fellow said, 'You can have it for nothing.' We pulled it out of his garage and towed it into town. I put it in gear but it just smoked the clutch, so I took it home and parked it in the driveway beside the other one."

With Jerry's two clunkers alongside the regular family car, the Shusters were now a three-car family, not uncommon today but definitely something to boast about in Leamington in the 1950s. And two of the three had current plates (the one he got for nothing had been off the road for a while and the plates had expired).

Jerry stood back and looked at his two cars sitting in the driveway. "Then I said to myself, 'Gee, this car I got for nothing looks better than the first one.' So I took the plates off the first car and put them on the second."

But it still didn't run.

"I took the head off the second car because the engine was seized, bought new valves, did all the valve polishing myself, poured penetrating oil into each cylinder, put the head back on with the gasket, my dad dragged me around the block behind his car with the clutch smoking — then all of a sudden *va-va-voom*! It took right off!"

September soon rolled around, and it was time to return to U of T for Jerry's second year of Engineering. And this time he drove there in his 1936 Chevy (the one he got for nothing), along with his good friend Tom Vodarek, also a student at U of T. The old Chevy barrelled right along on Highway 401 (at least on those parts that were open — other sections were still under construction). "By this time it was leaking a lot of oil. It took a gallon of oil to get to Toronto. Then we found the brakes had stopped working, but we beetled around the city anyway. Tom would sit next to me and pull up on the hand brake while pulling on the lights …"

With the U of T campus in the heart of downtown Toronto, Jerry and Tom soon realized that parking spaces were hard to find. Jerry had boarded at different places the previous year and was now living on Walmer Road just west of Bloor and Spadina and only a short fifteen-minute walk to class. One day Jerry left his 1936 Chevy parked in front of a driveway on Walmer Road:

"It was parked illegally, and the police took it, so I went to the pound to pick it up. They wanted ten bucks, and the registration didn't match the licence plates, so I said 'I'll come back later' — and I left it there. And the other one I left at home, my dad gave it away, so I never saw those cars again."

CHAPTER TWENTY-SIX

MY FIRST CAR By Bernard Lalonde

While growing up in Kingsville, Ontario, my first car was a 1929 Model A Ford. A two-door coach with the roof cut off and the doors welded shut. I believe the back seat was out of a 1948 Ford and was somewhat elevated, making it excellent for touring. The exhaust was a straight pipe that exited under the passengers' running board. It was purchased in 1957 for the sum of $60, to be traded two years later on a new 1959 Vauxhall. The trade-in value was $35.

When we first acquired the car, it was covered with graffiti, and Dad, objecting to the wording that so graciously adorned the exterior, made us paint over it. With paintbrush in hand we set out to cover the graffiti but ended up painting the whole car in red metal

(Front row from driver's side) Bernard Lalonde, Michael Lalonde, and Bernadette Lalonde. (Back row from driver's side) Marie Lalonde, Robert Smith, and Vic Lucas. Photo taken along the Lake Erie shoreline in 1957.

paint purchased to paint the lawnmower. The car was a joint venture between my sister and myself. She bought the car and possessed the ownership, and I quickly laid claim to all the driving rights. She could drive it in a straight line, but when it came to turning and shifting she found it too difficult and suddenly I found myself to be enthroned as designated driver, much to my delight. My hands never left the wheel. It had power steering (the amount of power my arms could supply), and the brakes were defiantly mechanical. It didn't matter how much I pushed on them, they did very little, and I had to rely a lot on down shifting to slow up. My dad thought the car was a danger and a menace, giving him a new topic to complain about. He said it was as dangerous as a ladder with missing rungs, then would reitcrate by saying not just a few rungs, but all of them. I never let him drive it, for if he did I knew that the next morning there would be nothing to inhabit my parking spot along the side of the house. Dad, not wanting to admit that he raised children not able to make good judgment, told his friends that we were conned by a travelling salesman into buying what was thought to be a late model car, but turned out to be otherwise. I don't think they bought it, and the truth of the matter was that we loved our first car. The whitewall tires were a great touch, and the swing-out front window gave the car great circulating air flow that was so refreshing when driving.

Driving it to school was great. I think I was in Grade 10. Come time to leave, I had to run like hell to get a seat. Not only was the car full but also the running boards. People would hang off this thing from everywhere. I remember one time my friend Vic Lucas and I drove back behind the football field to where there was a pear tree ripe for picking. Parking under it we shook the tree till we had a load of pears, then drove up and down the main street throwing pears at everyone walking home from school. We thought this was great fun until we were approached by someone of higher authority, namely the school principal. He instructed us to retrace our steps and pick up every pear we had thrown and return them to their place of origin. It was still fun.

I remember one day at the bottom of a steep incline I made my passengers get out of the car to lighten the load and walk their way to the top of the hill. I drove up and once at the top they were allowed to re-board and we resumed our journey. There was a lot of complaining, but still I was the captain of the ship and what I said went. One of the unique features of this prelude to modern transportation was its lack of power, but we didn't care, all we wanted was to feel the rush of air through our hair and the gasp for air at high speeds (30 miles per hour).

We loved waving at all our friends as we passed by, shouting unrestricted and sticking our hands in the air fighting off the wind resistance. It was a summer car and the days were long allowing extra driving time because those six-volt headlamps barely illuminated anything beyond the hand crank. Oh yes, the hand crank, a crooked metal hand crank that inserted into a hole at the bottom of the radiator. The crank would insert into the front of the engine's front fan belt pulley wheel with a one-way hook allowing the crank to latch on and turn in one direction. If you cranked it, you would turn the engine over enough to start it if the battery was dead or not strong enough to do it on its own. Dad always warned me, "Be careful, son, if that engine decides to backfire when you are cranking, it can send that crank backwards and break your arm." There was a special technique to "crank and release," and you wanted to make sure that was one of the first things you learned about this car. My first backfire didn't break my arm, but it did send a jolt up to my elbow that I still remember to this day.

The car didn't go fast but could reach 45 miles per hour if pushed. The engine would scream, and I believe to this day that one time after doing just that I turned it off and could hear it moan from pain. But it survived to run another day, and that's when I began to consider a proposal made to me by one of the townsfolk (who turned out to be, many years later, an uncle by marriage). This man was building a steel boat inside his garage. All hand-welded joints and would sleep several people. The question I had was how he would get this boat out when it was finished. It reached clear up into the rafters, and there was more to add to it. He explained that he wanted the engine from my car to put into his boat because the motor was so designed that it could run on diesel fuel with slight modifications to the carb. He had a flathead V8 engine that he would put into my car in exchange for my four-cylinder engine. He would do all the work. I thought this was great and it would give me the extra power I was looking for. My dad could give an all new meaning to the word *no*, and he did.

Living close to Point Pelee Park it was natural to spend a lot of time within its gates. Once inside and off the main road there were sand dunes. These were hills of sand covered with weeds, brush and lots of trees. The hills weren't large but steep and cars had a lot of tight turns to navigate. If you weren't careful you could scrape a tree with the fenders and running boards. No harm done, but if you went too fast and didn't quite manage to keep on course you might hit a tree head on. When this happened, and it did, we weren't going very fast and the spring steel bumpers were made to bounce back. They bounced with enough jolt to knock your false teeth out, if you had any. This was unbelievable fun. On one occasion while driving the dunes we crested one with too much speed and came down on the other side slightly airborne and with a thud. Then the car came to a stop. Getting out to examine it, I noticed a trail of water behind the car. The battery mounted under the floor boards had broken loose and bounced along the ground while being held by only one cable. The concussion punched a large hole in the side of the battery, allowing it to lose all of its water. No problem, we would have it fixed in no time. A piece of branch held the battery back in its place, we reconnected the dislodged cable, a mud pack and a piece of string held the battery patch in place, and then after filling it with lake water, away we went for more fun.

That old car gave us unforgettable memories and led to my second car, a 1929 Ford roadster pickup. It had no doors and the top was missing. That old pickup has as many summer stories as my first car, which I will always remember.

CHAPTER TWENTY-SEVEN:

JIM DOMM REMEMBERS DAD'S 1954 MONARCH LUCERNE

Jim Domm poses with pride over fifty years ago alongside the new 1954 Monarch Lucerne four-door sedan he persuaded his father, Earl Domm, to buy at Lawrence Motors in North Toronto. Jim is wearing his officer's uniform from the cadet corps at his high school, University of Toronto Schools. The car was light blue and is seen here in the family driveway at 22 Buckingham Avenue, in Toronto.

Jim Domm was born in Toronto on Sunday, November 29, 1936, and grew up in the family home at 22 Buckingham Avenue with his older sister, Georgianna, and their two parents, Earl and Mabel Domm. Of all the cars that have passed through the family from that day to this, one car in particular occupies a special place in Jim's heart: Dad's brand new 1954 Monarch Lucerne four-door sedan with whitewall tires, fender skirts, and blue and yellow interior.

Let's trace the chain of events leading to the purchase of that Monarch.

The first family car Jim can remember riding in was Dad's tan-brown 1942 Dodge coupe, which was probably purchased in the fall of 1941, when Jim turned five. That car carried the family all through the war.

After the war, Earl Domm needed a new car badly, and he probably would have bought another Dodge (or DeSoto), but Century Motors at 637 Yonge Street south of Bloor in mid-town Toronto could get him a new car sooner. Jim clearly remembers the new 1946 Hudson Super Six his dad purchased. It was black, and because it was among the first post-war cars, it was missing some parts: no back seat, no knob on the end of the column-mounted gearshift lever, and no steel bumpers (wooden bumpers were mounted in their place). The missing parts were on back order and were installed by the dealer as soon as they came in. The bumpers took several months to arrive.

Until that happy day, the Domm family had to improvise when driving north to their cottage in Barrillia Park near Oro Station on Lake Simcoe. Jim and his sister had to sit on folding lawn chairs for a back seat.

The original black factory finish on his 1946 Hudson prompted Earl just one year later to repaint the car himself with a spray gun on the front lawn of the family cottage.

Earl's next car was a 1949 Dodge Custom four-door sedan with fluid drive. It got a lot of use because Earl was on the road so much, usually away from home about eight days out of every ten business days.

Jim turned fifteen on Thursday, November 29, 1951. Back then, you could get a restricted driver's licence that allowed you to drive only your parents' car. Jim got his learner's permit right away, then drove with his dad to all his industrial accounts during the Christmas holidays, Easter break, and summer vacation. Earl enjoyed having Jim along, as now he had company on those long drives — and a chauffeur too. Jim liked it because his dad took him all over southern Ontario: "I remember staying at the William Pitt Hotel in downtown Chatham, then being treated to a tour of the International Harvester plant. It was great fun. I had a ball."

Jim's dad bought this light green 1949 Dodge with fluid drive brand new and drove it for three years. Jim is second from right and his sister Georgianna second from left.

They did this all through 1952 in Earl's 1949 Dodge. He bought it new at Hyland Motors at Yonge and Blytheswood from Harold Somerville, whose son Bill today owns Somerville National Leasing in Toronto.

Earl later traded in the light green 1949 Dodge on a dark blue 1951 Mercury four-door sedan at Yonge-Eglinton Motors. He probably knew someone there because he belonged to the North Toronto Kiwanis Club just around the corner from the dealership.

That Merc covered a lot of miles in the three years it was in the family — Earl drove it, Jim drove it, and Jim's sister, Georgianna, drove it. The driver's seat gradually developed a big sag and Jim stuffed it with kapok (from boat cushions).

By 1953, Jim was sixteen going on seventeen and wanted a car of his own. He announced one day that he would like to buy an old wreck and fix it up. "My dad freaked out when he heard this," recalls Jim. "Within forty-eight hours, he visited Elgin Motors at University and Front and bought a 1953 Ford Customline two-door (one of the cheapest Fords you could buy). It had a cream finish but no trim around the windows, no radio, standard shift — I think it may have had a heater."

And thus the Domms became a two-car family. Jim really didn't want to buy an old wreck, but figured if he said he did, his dad would buy a second car.

At first, Earl kept driving the Mercury and gave the Ford to Jim and Georgianna. But the Merc (now with high mileage) began showing signs of old age, so Earl began driving the Ford with Jim and Georgianna left to struggle along with the 1951 Merc.

By 1954, the Merc had to go. Earl took it to Lawrence Motors at the old city limits on Yonge just north of Glen Echo, and traded it in on a new Monarch Lucerne.

Jim drove the Merc there while his dad followed in the 1953 Ford. By this time, four inches of kapok had been stuffed under the seat of the Merc. Jim removed it before driving to the dealer — and the sag in the seat was so bad, Jim could barely see over the steering wheel.

Jim Domm smiles from behind the wheel of an unrestored 1954 Monarch in 2001. It needed a lot of work, and he decided not to buy it.

Earl wasn't sorry to see the last of that 1951 Merc, and Jim remembers why. "My father ripped those suicide doors off the car so many times by driving it into the garage. He'd leave a door open and forget. Then … *bang!* The air was always blue after that — the same colour as the car."

Jim made a point of going with his dad to Lawrence Motors to talk him into buying the most expensive model they had. They looked through the Monarch sales catalogue, and Jim tried to persuade his dad to spring for a new convertible. Earl turned that down flat because "a convertible wouldn't look right parked in front of Eglinton United Church on Sunday morning." But Jim did persuade his dad to go for the top-of-the-line 1954 Monarch sedan. It had to be ordered from the factory — and its arrival was a red-letter day in the Domm driveway. It was a powder blue 1954 Monarch Lucerne four-door with wide whitewalls, automatic transmission, full wheel covers, fender skirts, and a blue and yellow interior. It was the first luxurious car Earl had ever bought. Soon after buying it, he turned it into a two-tone by trotting out his spray gun again at the cottage and painting the roof of the Monarch a dark blue that contrasted nicely with the powder blue body.

Jim still had another year to go in high school, and he enjoyed driving the Monarch to various school functions and out on dates. "Girls weren't impressed with old cars," Jim recalls. "They liked being driven around in a new car." Jim had occasional access to the Monarch but only under special arrangement. He could borrow the car from time to time as long as he washed it every Sunday morning in time for church.

Earl's 1954 Monarch was equipped with factory-original flush-mounted fender skirts. To clean the whitewalls, Jim at first removed the skirts, then had great difficulty getting them back on because a metal lever had to be jammed up into place. On the next wash job, he soaped half the tire, then moved the car ahead to clean the other half. The skirt covered half the tire, and Earl could see the ridge of dirt where the two halves touched. After that, Jim cleaned the rear whitewalls one-third at a time.

Earl always parked in the same place every Sunday at Eglinton United Church on Sheldrake Boulevard, and the family always sat in the same pew.

Earl's 1953 Ford was finally traded in at Lawrence Motors for a new, dark blue 1956 Ford two-door with V8 and stick shift. "You put it in low, then stepped on the gas and *whoooosh*!" recalls Jim. "I burned a lot of rubber with that baby!"

The next day, Jim had a ride in Alistair Kielly's fully restored 1954 Monarch Lucerne four-door sedan. Jim was tempted to buy it, but it wasn't for sale.

Meanwhile, Jim and Georgianna continued to share the 1954 Monarch — and Jim kept driving it even after he got married. Then his wife acquired a VW Beetle. They shared the use of it, and the 1954 Monarch Lucerne was finally sold.

In preparing this story, I asked Jim if he remembered any other cars while he was growing up at 22 Buckingham Avenue in the Lawrence Park area. "I was an enterprising kid," recalled Jim. "John Hartill lived across the street, and he and I started a car washing business on Buckingham Avenue. We were thirteen or fourteen at the time, and we charged a dollar a car. It wasn't so much that we liked washing cars or wanted the money — but the cars had to be washed in *our* driveway. That way, we got to drive the cars at least half a block to our driveway — and that's why we started our car washing business.

"Mayor Saunders lived five houses down the street, at 42 Buckingham Ave. He had a light green 1953 Oldsmobile that was on display at the CNE, where he bought it. It had automatic windows — power everything! — and we got to drive it five houses down to our driveway. John and I took turns — he'd drive it one way and I'd drive it the other.

"Our street was always the first one ploughed after a snow storm. It helped, having the mayor five doors away.

"We often washed fifteen or sixteen cars on a Saturday. The last car we washed was Dad's 1954 Monarch Lucerne for church Sunday morning. And that was a freebie. No dollar. But it guaranteed me a free ride to church."

Now roll the clock ahead some forty years. Jim by then was related to me (his father, Earl, married my mother, Edna, in 1978, six years after their respective spouses had passed away). And even by the year 2001, Earl's 1954 Monarch Lucerne still occupied a special place in Jim's heart. He began thinking of buying one.

I found two of them for him to look at. One was near Peterborough, and we looked at that one first. The price seemed reasonable, but it needed a lot of work, and Jim decided to give it a pass. The next day, we had a ride in a beautifully restored 1954 Monarch Lucerne four-door sedan owned by Alistair Kielly in Scarborough, Ontario. Jim fell in love with it, but it wasn't for sale. Jim is still looking …

CHAPTER TWENTY-EIGHT:

EARL DOMM MEETS RON FAWCETT

Pierce-Arrow … The very name evokes an aura of incredible luxury and uncompromising quality. For more than a third of a century, from 1901 to 1938, the company founded by George Pierce produced some of America's most revered automotive classics. Yet until 1978, Pierce-Arrow to me was simply another make of car that was no longer in business.

Then in February of that year, my mother, a widow, married Earl Domm, a widower. And that's when I discovered that my new stepfather had once worked for Pierce-Arrow in Buffalo, New York!

Another thirteen years would roll by before I got around to putting Earl's story

Earl Domm and Ron Fawcett posed for this picture on July 1, 1988, in the front seat of Ron's 1918 Pierce-Arrow seven-passenger touring after their ride on the highway. Ron did the driving but insisted that Earl sit behind the wheel for the photo. Right-hand-drive was retained by Pierce-Arrow until 1920.

on paper. What you are about to read was told to me by my step-father on Monday, December 16, 1991, the day he turned eighty-nine.

Earl Domm was born in Ayton, Ontario, in 1902, and grew up in the middle of the Model T Ford era. He could still recall seeing freight trains pull into town with Model T chassis on flatcars and Model T bodies in boxcars. These would be unloaded onto the station platform, where the local Ford dealer would bolt the bodies onto the chassis, then drive the assembled cars to his dealership (and you thought kit cars were something new!).

In 1925, Earl graduated from the University of Toronto with a degree in Chemical Engineering and spent his working life in the paint business, eventually becoming chief chemist for the Imperial Paint Company in Toronto.

In 1928, Earl had the opportunity to test his talents in international waters when he landed a job at the Pierce-Arrow factory in Buffalo. Unfortunately, Pierce-Arrow had been having financial difficulties at that time and had just been taken over by the Studebaker Corporation of South Bend, Indiana. The old-timers at Pierce-Arrow resented all newcomers at that time, including Earl.

Earl was responsible for the quality of the paint on every Pierce-Arrow that rolled off the assembly line, and his office was right next to that part of the factory where the headlights were mounted onto the front fenders — a styling trademark started by Pierce-Arrow in 1913 and finally adopted by other American cars more than twenty years later. Each headlight housing had to be hammer-welded onto each fender, and Earl said the noise was deafening. In fact, he claimed he could still hear the pounding of those hammers on the fenders over sixty years later!

While working in Buffalo, Earl stayed at a boarding house run by a lady named Aunt Ell, whose brother, Mr. Bull, operated a Pierce-Arrow dealership in the city. Every Labour Day weekend, Mr. Bull would send a chauffeur-driven Pierce-Arrow sedan over to Aunt Ell's place to take her and all her boarders on a motor trip. Earl travelled with them one year to Chicago and another year to New England.

Aunt Ell was always careful to get good value for her money. Earl can still remember the day they were rolling down the main street of Montpelier, Vermont, when the chauffeur spotted a nice tourist home for the night (this was in the days before motels). He was about to turn in to the driveway when Aunt Ell said, "Keep going and pull around the corner. I'll walk back and see how much they charge. If they see us pull up in a Pierce-Arrow, they'll want too much money." The average tourist home that Earl stayed in back then charged a dollar a night.

Earl often travelled back to Toronto on weekends and often got a ride with a Toronto friend named Guy Winter, who also worked in Buffalo.

Guy owned a very sporty green 1927 Essex boattail speedster that had enough power to get them up the big, long hill at Lewiston, New York, without shifting out of high gear. Sometimes they would park the Essex in a friend's garage in Lewiston and take the *Cayuga*, a lake ferry, back to Toronto.

Sometimes, on the return journey, when the weather was bad, they would leave the Essex where it was and take the Gorge railway to Niagara Falls. The tracks clung to a shelf of rock just above the raging waters of the Niagara River, and on one particularly stormy night, they could hear mud and gravel falling onto the roof of the train. Then the train had to stop because a big boulder had landed on the tracks up ahead. The passengers had to climb out and push it into the river before the train could proceed. I wonder if the folks at Pierce-Arrow realized Earl was risking life and limb to keep those cars rolling out of the factory.

When Earl finally left the company, the Great Depression was underway and production at Pierce-Arrow had fallen to six cars a day. Studebaker pulled out in 1933, but a group of Buffalo businessmen took over and tried valiantly to keep the company afloat. What they needed was $11 million, but they didn't have it and couldn't get it. The remnants of the company were finally auctioned off for a mere $40,000 on Friday, May 13, 1938.

Fifty years after the company folded, Pierce-Arrow once again came back into Earl's life when I drove him and my mother to visit Ron and Huguette Fawcett at their home north of Whitby, Ontario, on July 1, 1988. It was the first time Ron and Earl had met, and they became instant friends. The highlight of the visit for Earl was a ride on the highway in Ron's fully restored 1918 Pierce-Arrow seven-passenger touring.

Earl was so thrilled by his ride in Ron's car that he invited Ron and Huguette to my mother's house in Toronto later that summer. And when they arrived, Earl presented Ron with several Pierce-Arrow pinstripers that Earl had saved from the days he was at the factory. All the pinstriping back then was done with these tools with their little rollers, and the men who did this work had very steady hands. They then trained younger men to take over when they got too old. The letters "P-A" are stamped on each pinstriper, and each new Pierce-Arrow had pin-striping applied to the wheels and fenders and body.

Now, when Ron restores a Pierce-Arrow, he is able to pinstripe the car with the same striping tools used on the car in the factory when the car was new. Earl was very pleased to have made this possible.

This story was first published in *Old Autos* newspaper on Monday, February 3, 1992. Earl Domm passed away in the summer of 1994 at the age of ninety-one. I am grateful that I had the opportunity to hear his story while he was still with us.

This is the Pierce-Arrow sedan used by Earl's landlady in Buffalo. She took her boarders on many weekend excursions in this car.

CHAPTER TWENTY-NINE:

OLD ESSEX ROADSTER FOR $25

On a recent visit to Toronto, I stopped in to see Jack and Jean Morton at their home on Pemberton Avenue. Jack has been active in the old car hobby for over fifty years, and I've known him since October 1959, when we each displayed a car at the first Fort York Armoury Autorama. Jack was there with his all-original 1927 Model T Ford coupe, and my brother John and I displayed our all-original 1940 Buick Super coupe.

On my most recent visit to Jack's home in the spring of 2004, he handed me an envelope containing the photo you see here. On the back are written these words: "About 1946. Essex roadster bought for $25 but it had no tires by Lou Turner. Photo taken at Stefaroi's house on Passmore Ave. east of Kennedy Rd., east side train tracks."

A close look at the photo reveals some interesting details. If the photo was taken in "about 1946," the car had been off the road for several years, judging by the white-on-black 1939 front plate. A cluster of little flags can be seen sticking up from the rad cap — a common dress-up feature on cars back then. And the front tires are not completely bald, suggesting that the car might still have a few miles left in it yet. The

grille and rad shell confirm that this car is indeed an Essex roadster, a 1928, 1929, or 1930 model (there were very few changes for those three years).

The Essex first appeared in 1919 as a moderately priced car built by the Hudson Motor Car Co. of Detroit, Michigan. Beginning in February 1932, Hudson and Essex cars were produced in Tilbury, Ontario, to supply the nearly six hundred dealers across Canada.

CHAPTER THIRTY:

1932 CHEVROLET ROADSTER WITH CANOE

David Laverie of Osgoode, Ontario, wrote: "The photo of the car and canoe was taken on a farm at Haley Station, Ontario. My father had rented the farm for the summer so Mother and I could stay there while he worked on a construction site nearby. My mother's Uncle Henry and Aunt Eileen (avid fishermen) came to visit for the weekend from Ottawa. There was a lake on the farm that was full of bass and pike, so the fishing contest was on!

"The two photos were taken around 1948. In the first photo (left to right), my grandmother, Mary Hawkins, my mother's Uncle Henry Hawkins, my dad, Bill Laverie, my mother, Eileen Laverie, holding Tiny, my dog, and that's me, David Laverie, in front, about eight years old. In the second photo, Aunt Eileen Hawkins is sitting on the car."

When these photos were taken, the car was already sixteen years old and probably worth less than a hundred dollars on the used car market. Today, a restored 1932 Chevy roadster is worth more than some new cars.

The roadster shown here was powered by the overhead-valve six-cylinder engine first introduced by Chevrolet in 1929 in response to Henry Ford's four-cylinder Model A introduced the previous year.

Henry was not happy with his chief rival having two extra cylinders under the hood, and he decided to do something about it. He couldn't take action right away because his new Model A was only in its second year of production, and he needed time to develop his answer to the six-cylinder Chevrolet.

The answer came in March 1932, when Ford introduced the first V8 engine in the low-priced field. To keep down the cost of production, the V8 engine block had to be cast in a single piece — and many so-called experts said it couldn't be done.

Henry pressed ahead regardless, and spent $300 million of his own money to make his new V8 engine a reality. The first hundred or so blocks had to be scrapped before production could begin. The new 1932 Ford was a mechanical and styling sensation — and the new flathead V8 engine remained in production (with some ongoing changes) up to 1953 in the United States and 1954 in Canada.

But Chevrolet still held the sales lead in 1932, and in every other year of the 1930s except 1935. The 1932 Chevy roadster shown here was a good-looking, well-built car, popular when new and still popular today.

CHAPTER THIRTY-ONE:

TWO OLD PHOTOS FROM ESSEX COUNTY

Rudy Spitse of Ruthven, Ontario, recently passed along these two old photos to the Old Car Detective. In the upper photo, his mother is holding him on the hood of a 1935 Ford with a 1951 plate (844NX). Rudy was about one year old at the time. The car has an accessory grille guard and has been converted to sealed-beam headlights. Judging by the snow on the ground, the photo was apparently taken in winter. Historically, 1935 is noteworthy in representing the only year in the 1930s when Ford outsold Chevrolet.

The second photo was taken two years after the first, judging by the 1953 Ontario plate on the front of the car. Now about three years old and no longer needing his mother to steady him, Rudy is standing on the bumper supports and leaning against the hood.

The car itself is a 1940 Mercury with a bold, striking, two-tone aftermarket repaint job. Note also the outside sun visor, tall cowl-mounted radio aerial, and off-centre licence plate apparently held in place by a single bolt. The crank hole cover in the lower grille is open, suggesting that this car might have needed a crank. Rust is already apparent on the lower portion of the driver's-side headlight bezel and no doubt has gained a foothold elsewhere on the car.

Most 1940 Mercurys made it to 1950 because they were driven very little during the war years. But time, and rust, take their toll, and most cars built in Canada in 1940 had been scrapped by 1960.

Rudy does not remember who owned these cars, and apparently no one now living has any knowledge of them either. They were photographed somewhere in Essex County, Ontario, in the early 1950s. The story behind them has disappeared.

GORD HARSELL'S 1941 MERCURY CONVERTIBLE By Gord Harsell

*Gord Harsell's words below were included in a story I wrote
about his first car for Old Autos newspaper, December 3, 2001.*

I purchased my first red 1941 Mercury convertible in Leaskdale, Ontario, in 1952. Leaskdale is about six miles north of Uxbridge with one small garage, one church, one general store, and one used car lot, with a population of fifty or sixty people. I don't recall the name of the car lot or the person who ran it, nor the price of the car — maybe about $300, which was a very high price for a car at that time. But convertibles (except for Model T's) were in short supply, and age sixteen only comes once.

Gord Harsell is holding the hood from his very first car, the 1941 Mercury convertible he sold fifty years earlier. This is all that's left of that car. Gord is pointing to the hole he drilled in the hood more than fifty years ago to install a big chrome-plated swan hood ornament, a popular accessory in those days.

At that time my only expenses were clothes and gasoline, about twenty-eight cents a gallon, two dollars' worth would last all week and about five dollars' worth on weekends.

Looking back, it seems my only activities were working at GM in Oshawa, driving around in my car, going to shows through the week and to dances all around the area on the weekends. What a time to have a convertible! Tailor-made clothes, an abundance of pretty young ladies, and money in your pocket. The memories are probably far better than the reality, but I had fun!!!

I drove this car for two years, and friends recall that in the winter, snow blew in through the top of the windshield. In the summer there was much windburn on the back of my neck because I had the top down even when it was cold. The joys of having a convertible!

This is what Gord Harsell found in Wisconsin after his retirement in 1997. From these pitiful remains, he is now bringing two 1941 Mercury convertibles back to life.

I sold this car in 1954 to Bill Morgan, who ran a garage in Uxbridge, where I lived. His nephew from Toronto fixed it up and repainted it yellow and black, added a continental on the back, and sold it to Bill Barton of Uxbridge. Bill drove the car for several years, then sold it to Mark Smith's Auto Wreckers in Udora, Ontario, where it sat for some time until someone from Port Perry bought it. Since then, neither Bill Barton nor I can find any trace of the car. No pictures that we know of survived, so all trace is lost.

In this story, I described Gord's search for another 1941 Mercury convertible after his retirement in 1997. In Elroy, Wisconsin, he found the pitiful remains of a 1941 Mercury convertible with almost enough spare parts to build two. And that's what he's doing — restoring one to original and building the other as a street rod, with help from fellow 1941 Mercury enthusiasts in Ohio and as far away as Indonesia. When the story of Gord's original 1941 was published, we had our fingers crossed, hoping the car had survived the last fifty years and that we could find it. Well, most of the car is gone, but the hood still exists, and here is Gord's report.

Loaded up and leaving Wisconsin for Ontario. Gord's memories of his first car are about to come alive once more.

Noel Hamer of Odessa, Ontario, (well known in the old car hobby) called and told me that in 1967 he bought a door for a 1941 Mercury convertible from a man named Charnochan who lived south of Port Perry. Noel told me there was not much left of the car at that time. I called all the Charnochans in the phone book and finally talked to George Charnochan.

For years George's brother Jim bought interesting cars and parts from various locations around the area and brought them to the farm, and some parts he used and some parts he didn't, so some parts stayed around the farm for years. George told me when Jim bought the 1941 Mercury convertible from Harold Harding's wrecking yard (formerly Mark Smith's) in Udora, there was little left of it. The top mechanism, the right door, the trunk lid, and most of the stainless steel were missing. George informed me that he still had the hood from that car, which had lain in the barnyard for many years, and that was all that was left of the car, as many years before they had taken most of the cars and parts to the junkyard to clean up the farm.

I went to see the hood, and sure enough it was from my original Mercury. It was in very bad shape, but I wanted to buy it for nostalgia's sake to use on the car I am now building even though it will cost far more to restore than the hood is worth. George would take no money for the hood as he felt that I should have it free of charge since it meant so much to me.

In the picture of the hood I am pointing to some holes that I drilled with a hand twist drill in the hot sun to mount a silver swan, which was all the rage at that time. If not for *Old Autos* newspaper and Bill Sherk, I would never have known what happened to my old car nor have the hood in my possession. For this I am very thankful.

It should be noted that Gord Harsell has found other owners of 1941 Mercury convertibles in Canada and the United States — and a rare right-hand-drive, Canadian-built, Singapore-assembled 1941 Mercury convertible owned by Kevin White in Bali. And all this excitement because of the car he bought in 1952 when he was sixteen. And what memories!

In your teenage years with a convertible, girls as well as cars play a very big part in your life. I was possibly heading for the wilder side of life when I met Isobell. We went to various places such as Sunnyside and the Markham Fair for a year or so. Of course, when you have a car that is known in a wide area and you go steady with one girl, then someone sees you with another girl in your car, trouble happens and you find you no longer have a steady girlfriend.

My next steady girl, Elaine, had my undivided attention for several years, and we were an item. She outlasted the car, and we had many fun times together. I don't foresee changing my affection for old cars, but I would sell them all if it would buy me a few weeks of fun that I was fortunate enough to have in the early 1950s.

On September 12, 2004, Gord parked his newly restored 1941 Mercury convertible at 81 Victoria Drive in Uxbridge, Ontario, where his first 1941 convertible would have been parked many times fifty years ago. Gord's parents lived in that house from 1945 to 1986.

CHAPTER THIRTY-THREE:

DAVID WELLS' AUTOMOTIVE MEMORIES By David Wells

David Wells of Sechelt, British Columbia, wrote the following letter to the
Old Car Detective on February 16, 2004.

Dear Bill Sherk,

I really enjoyed your book *60 Years Behind the Wheel*. Here I am in 1950 in my 1934 Plymouth, suicide doors and all. The car was powered by "floating power," an in-line flat-head six. It featured "free wheeling." When you pulled out a knob on the dash, the motor was disconnected from the transmission, and the car coasted when you took your foot off the gas pedal, saving gas (this at nineteen cents a gallon!).

Dig all that chrome. And this on a standard model. Notice the crank slot in the grille and the Canadian Tire fog lights on either side of it. Notice too the *one* windshield wiper, which would stop if you floored the gas (vacuum operated).

There was a small crank on the dash that raised the windshield up and out. Notice the vent on the back quarter panel and the vent on the front doors. By the time you opened all these, you didn't need air conditioning. But I installed a "south wind" gas heater for those cold days. Notice too the sealed-beam kits on the lights.

The spare was on the back. Looks like the left front tire could use it! My dad and I both had the same car, both in good shape, but he couldn't drive.

I seemed to choose odd cars. See the Corvair station wagon powered in the rear by an air-cooled six-cylinder Franklin aircraft engine. These Corvairs were notorious for spinning. Those cars spun! My wife, daughter, and I made a hurried trip from Toronto to LaGuardia for a Christmas 1968 flight to Barbados. We dashed off to catch the flight but couldn't find the keys! No matter. Corvairs ran without a key if it was not in "lock." My wife drove while travelling through the mountains of Pennsylvania. "David! Wake up!" We were spinning. *Bang!!* went the back corner against the guard rail. *Bang!!* went the front corner against the guard rail. Good thing; it was a long way down. Now the fender was rubbing against the front tire. Couldn't turn!

We made it to a key shop in Trenton to get a key to open the front trunk. The owner handed me a huge ring and said, "Try these." And one did work. We continued on to a superb trip and a three-room walled villa for ten dollars a day. The car in the photo is all fixed. I sold it the next day.

More oddball cars I bought. That's my wife and daughter in a 1961 (?) N.S.U. Prinz. The name is on the fender. I thought I bought the only one, but a friend told me when his dad bought his first car, it was an N.S.U. Prinz.

Finally, an overhead shot of a 1961 Studebaker. My wife and I put in rings and bearings right where you see it, on a gravel parking lot. This car rusted out, and I sold it in 1964.

CHAPTER THIRTY-FOUR:

BOB JAMES' FIRST CAR: A 1938 PLYMOUTH

The following story was first published in Old Autos *newspaper on May 16, 1994.*

If you have been in the old car hobby for some time now you certainly know Bob James, a guy with a smile and a heart as big as the whole outdoors.

I first met Bob back in 1971, when he was busy organizing a cavalcade of McLaughlin-Buicks in Oshawa to celebrate the one-hundredth birthday of Colonel Sam McLaughlin, founder of General Motors of Canada. About fifty cars were lined up and ready to roll through the circular driveway of Parkwood, the home of Colonel Sam — who was sitting outside his front door, ready to wave at all the cars poised to glide past him.

As parade marshall, Bob James gave us strict orders not to rev the engine or blow the horn or lean out the windows and shout "Happy birthday" while we drove past the granddaddy of the Canadian automotive industry. Bob was just making sure that the colonel would still be there when the last car passed by.

Bob's words of caution were well heeded and produced the desired results. The parade held in June of 1971 came off without a hitch, and Colonel Sam turned one hundred that September. He died peacefully in his sleep the following January.

As a legacy to his memory, the McLaughlin-Buick Club of Canada had been created the previous summer, when Colonel Sam was still

It's early 1952 in Montreal and a youthful Bob James strikes a pride-of-ownership pose with his very first car: a 1938 Plymouth coach. The 1948 Pontiac Silver-streak in the background belonged to a German family who lived above Bob. They later repainted their car "Oshawa Blue" right outside their home with a vacuum cleaner.

alive. Bob James was a driving force behind the formation of the club, which is still flourishing today.

One of my favourite questions to ask other old car nuts is this one: "What do you remember about your very first car?" When I put this question to Bob James, it triggered an avalanche of memories and several hours of fascinating conversation. Bob first became a car owner more than fifty years ago, but he can still recall the details of his early cars as if he had owned them yesterday. He has an album full of old photos of all his early cars going back to 1952. And — now get this! — he also has a file folder for each car with all the receipts for all the repairs and servicing performed on each car! (The prices will make you weep.) So settle into your favourite easy chair and read on …

Bob James was born in Montreal on January 28, 1934. When he was ten years old, Bob moved with his family to a town near the Gaspé coast — and it was here that Bob learned to speak fluent French. The family moved back to Montreal in June of 1951. Bob by now was seventeen and itching to buy a car.

He found his first car in the fall of 1951 at the Favor Brothers used car lot at Addington and Sherbrooke streets (N.D.G.) Three brothers ran this lot and bought cars wholesale from Hart Motors, a Mercury-Lincoln-Meteor dealership where Bob's father worked (the dealership was located near the airport at Dorval).

I wrote Bob's 1938 Plymouth story for Old Autos in 1994. Here we are at a car show in Waterdown, Ontario, and I am presenting to Bob (he's on the right) the issue of Old Autos in which his story was published. Since then, Bob has supplied me with other great stories (see pages 25 and 51).

One of the cars sitting on the Favor Brothers lot was a dark blue 1938 Plymouth coach in good original condition with serial #9353916 (does anyone own this car today?). The sticker price was $325, and Bob was determined to buy it. He was working in the parts department at International Harvester at the time and cleared $64 every two weeks. From that, he took $25, hopped aboard a streetcar, and made another payment toward the Plymouth.

The deal was set up so that when the car was half paid for, Bob could take possession of it. It was a proud day in March of 1952 when Bob slid behind the wheel and drove home in his very first car! He had just turned eighteen.

Keeping up the payments of $25 every two weeks suddenly became much more difficult because Bob now had the cost of running the car eating into his budget. Many a night out on the town, he had to push the car home because he ran out of gas. But despite the squeeze on his wallet, Bob did manage to install a radio under the dash — and he still has the receipt from Hart Motors for the mounting brackets ($1.50 on June 2, 1952). Now Bob had a car tailor-made for romance with a radio that played music when he ran out of gas. My oh my, if that back seat could talk!

While Bob was heading for a baseball game in the spring of 1952 along Upper Lachine Road, the Plymouth suddenly lost power. He turned off the key and pulled off the road in neutral (just as his dad had taught him to). With the car now stopped, Bob started the engine again. It fired up right away — but when he put the car in gear and tried to pull away, nothing happened. There was no power reaching the rear wheels.

Bob had the car towed to Fuller's Garage in Montreal West, where they discovered Bob's rear end had given out. The garage obtained a replacement rear end from nearby Vincent Auto Wreckers, who took the old differential in exchange. Bob still has the receipt, dated April 28, 1952, from "Ville St. Pierre Automobile Service Enr'g" at 101 Elm Avenue in Ville St. Pierre. The cost was $20 and no tax. The receipt also shows the car's mileage: 26,350 (and that's miles, not kilometres).

Another of Bob's repair bills shows up on Hart Motors repair order No. 9483, dated March 22, 1952. The description reads: "Check short under dash for lights. Check fuel gauge." The labour came to $2.00 and parts to $1.66. Tax of four cents brought the total to a whopping $3.70, which Bob paid on March 25. The fact that Bob's father worked at Hart Motors helped to keep those numbers down.

If you lived in Montreal in the early 1950s, you probably remember Modern Motor Sales Limited at 1400-1406 Dorchester Street West, specializing in Chrysler Corporation parts and accessories ("Largest Distributors for Eastern Canada"). Bob pulled in one day in his 1938 Plymouth and bought four wheel studs at sixteen cents apiece. Total bill: a staggering sixty-four cents.

Bruce James (no relation), Caryl A. Reynolds (his initials were C.A.R.), and Bob drove many times in the 1938 Plymouth to the driving range on Decarie Boulevard to hit some golf balls. On the way home one night, they ran out of gas, but they saw a Texaco station up ahead, and it was open. As they coasted in, the fellow inside was closing up for the night and turned out all the lights. Then he saw the Plymouth at the pumps and turned all the lights on again. Bob and his two buddies turned their pockets inside out and came up with a total of twenty-five cents. The man gave Bob a dirty look, then put in twenty-five cents' worth of gas — which got them home.

On another night, the three fellows ran out of gas on Sherbrooke Street and pushed the car to the edge of a hill, where it rolled down Elmhurst Avenue into the lane behind Bob's apartment.

In the summer of 1952, Bob, Bruce, and Caryl drove the Plymouth on a golfing trip around Lake Erie. Only one part fell off on the entire trip. They were driving along King Street in Oshawa at two in the morning (near the start of the trip) when the right rear hubcap came flying off and rolled out of sight. The boys stopped the car and climbed out. It was a residential neighbourhood, and all the houses were in darkness. The boys had to search all up and down the street before they found the hubcap in someone's flowerbed. If the police had driven by and spotted these three suspicious-looking characters, they might have spent the night in jail. They entered the United States by driving through the Detroit-Windsor Tunnel. On the far side, Bob was asked by a U.S. customs officer, "Is there any reason you should not be allowed into the United States?" Bob couldn't think of one, and they were waved on through. The boys played golf all around Lake Erie and often were allowed to play free or at a very nominal charge, thanks to Bruce being the assistant pro at the Grove Hill Golf Course in Lachine, Quebec (the golf course is now covered with houses and apartment buildings).

During this thirteen-hundred-mile trip, the boys noticed one day that the inner tube could be seen through a crack in the tread of one of the tires. Instead of changing it, they kept on going, following the old maxim, "If it ain't broke, don't fix it." They got all the way home without a flat.

In September of 1952, a 1941 Ford convertible was sitting on the used car lot of Decarie Motors. It was yellow with maroon fenders, and the price was $495. Bob was driving by one day in his 1938 Plymouth when he spotted the 1941 Ford and pulled in for a closer look. It was love at first sight — and that story is in this book! See page 51.

CHAPTER THIRTY-FIVE

JIM NEVISON'S 1951 FORD CONVERTIBLE *By Jim Nevison*

My first car was a 1951 Ford convertible purchased in mid-February 1954 from Evans Motors Ltd. on Bloor Street West in Etobicoke. I took delivery on Friday, February 19. I was the second owner. It was red with a black top and had approximately 70,000 miles on the odometer.

If I remember correctly, it cost around $1,500. That day, I went with my brothers and sister for a cold ride with the top down. Anyone seeing us must have thought we were crazy.

Right away I needed some front end repairs and new shock absorbers. But the car was reliable. The only repairs required later were a new fuel pump in June 1955 (it was a hot summer that year) and a trip to Thorncrest Motors on Dundas Street West to repair the convertible top mechanism later in the year.

The car remained as I bought it the first year. With car payments I had little money, but I did buy new tires for the front. The chrome plating was worn thin — typical Korean War. I had a new rear bumper after I was rear-ended. Unfortunately, I never did have the grille and front bumper replated.

In the spring of 1955, I made some changes, having more cash on hand by now. I finally bought new tires for the rear and added aftermarket trim rings, fender skirts, dual exhaust system with chrome extensions, Hollywood mufflers, and a radio. The car had a standard transmission (no overdrive).

The picture in the driveway (I'm in the car) was taken just after everything was completed. 1955 was a very good year. I turned twenty-one, lived in the Kingsway, and had a girlfriend who lived in North Toronto. We really enjoyed the convertible and drove it everywhere. This included trips to Niagara Falls, Queenston Heights, and Niagara-on-the-Lake with stops at Brock's Monument, the floral clock, and gardens by the Rainbow Bridge.

We enjoyed beautiful *hot* weather that summer. We travelled around Lake of Bays and to Algonquin Park. However there was one outing I wanted to forget. We went to Woodland beach, north of Wasaga on Georgian Bay, on a Sunday in July, and I got the worst sunburn of my life. Even the bottom of my feet were burned. A day later I had blisters the size of a fifty-cent piece all over me. When I went to the doctor, he ordered me to stay home for a week with all my bandages. This did not sit well with the medical group at Ford Motor Co. where I worked — self-inflicted injuries. My other passengers received only minor burns. I was told that if I were in the army I would have had my pay deducted.

One evening we had reserved seat tickets to *Oklahoma* with Shirley Jones and Gordon MacRae at the Tivoli in downtown Toronto. When we were about to leave my girlfriend's house she couldn't find the tickets. We searched for them and finally found them under a teapot warmer by the stove. Being late, it was the fastest trip I ever made. We were there in twenty minutes because she knew the best route downtown. We only missed the opening credits.

We went to Timothy Eaton United Church, on St. Clair Avenue West one Sunday evening. I parked the car on an adjacent side street with the top down and came back to find everything was still there — the good old days!

We were going to Buffalo to see *This is Cinerama* with another couple. The night before, Donna took my car home from my family's house. We lived at the top of a steep hill by the Humber River. She took off down the road. It was so dark I couldn't see the bottom. However, I did hear her sorting out the gears. I winced and cringed. She arrived the next day at the Ford plant with the top down by 5:00 p.m. to pick me up. We were on our way to Buffalo with me driving.

Other memories: On one warm evening we were with our girls, six of us, with the top folded singing along with Bill Haley and the Comets on the radio. The song was "Rock Around the Clock."

During this time we dated and double dated to places like Casa Loma (featuring Benny Lewis and his orchestra), Mart Kenny's Ranch, and the Brant Inn in Burlington.

To wrap up the year, we all went in several cars to Limberlost Ski Lodge near Lake of Bays for the New Year weekend. It was cold and dry, with the snow crunching under our winter boots. This weather was indeed invigorating but created battery problems. At nightfall we brought them into the chalet to keep them warm, all lined up in a row. When it came time to leave for home we still had difficulties starting the cars. Fortunately, one car was a 1954 or 1955 Buick, which had a twelve-volt system. We used it to boost our anemic six-volt batteries, ensuring that all lights including door closings, radio, and heaters, etc., were off — not recommended, to be sure, but it worked.

We had to share the inside of my car with the skis and poles because it was a convertible. Someone put the tip of a pole through the plastic rear window. Our wonderful weekend and a great year with my first car came to an end. I was really on top of the world driving my 1951 Ford convertible and still remember it well fifty years later.

Jim Nevison and his friend Jack Banks were photographed at the Ford Rotunda on the American Thanksgiving weekend in 1953 (Jim is on the left). They both worked for Ford of Canada in Oakville. The car is a 1953 Hudson Jet. It was a family car, Jim's dad being a "Hudson man" for years.

CHAPTER THIRTY-SIX

BOB AND MARION OMSTEAD'S 1949 FORD COUPE

This light grey 1949 Ford coupe was purchased in 1950 by Bob Omstead of Wheatley, Ontario, from his brother, Leonard R. Omstead, who bought it new from Jackson Motors, the local Ford dealer.

It was Bob's first car. He spiffed it up with a wind-shield sun visor and whitewall tires to take his new wife, Marion, on their honeymoon to Florida in February 1951. They drove all the way to Miami with no car trouble at all. In fact, the car made two trips to Florida during the four years they owned it. They eventually traded it in at Jackson Motors for a 1954 Ford.

In the photo with Bob leaning against the driver's door, the car already had a radio, aftermarket headlight eyebrows, and aftermarket portholes on the front fenders inspired by the 1949 Buicks.

The 1949 Fords actually went on sale as early as June 1948, as all the auto makers scrambled to deliver newly designed vehicles to replace the face-lifted pre-war cars available in 1946, 1947, and 1948. The 1949 Ford was three inches lower than the 1948 and totally different in style with a new slab-sided body, bold new grille, new dashboard, new bumpers, new tail lights, new door handles — the list goes on and on.

Mechanically there were significant changes. The faithful flathead V8 was still under the hood but power was now transmitted via an open driveshaft to a rear axle held in place by parallel longitudinal springs. Up front, the 1949 Ford boasted an independent front suspension.

When Bob and Marion drove their 1949 Ford on their honeymoon, they were just about up to date with everything else on the road.

CHAPTER THIRTY-SEVEN:

MURRAY MCDIARMID'S AUTOMOTIVE MEMORIES By Murray McDiarmid

On November 27, 2003, the following letter reached the Old Car Detective.

Dear Bill Sherk,

Congratulations on your new book *60 Years Behind the Wheel*. I liked it so well I purchased another copy for my brother as a Christmas gift.

I noticed in the back of the book your request for photographs of old cars for your second volume. Please find the following photos and text that you may be able to use.

Yours truly,

Murray McDiarmid,
Lakefield, Ontario

Murray included five nostalgic black and white photos of cars and trucks from days gone by along with his own reminiscences about them.

"This 1938 Hudson Terraplane pickup was purchased by my father, Harold McDiarmid, to drive back and forth to work. It was also used to carry his Rototiller to do custom tilling after work and weekends. Not the prettiest truck, but I did learn to drive with it."

"This 1940 Chevy was purchased new by my grandfather John Bray and used continuously until 1954 delivering eggs from the family farm between Raglan and Oshawa."

"This 1949 Morris Minor convertible was my first car, purchased while still in school at the Oshawa Collegiate and Vocational Institute. My younger brother Harvey is behind the wheel."

"My 1952 Ford coupe was one of my customs. The flathead V8 was equipped with a two-carb manifold, Mallory distributor, and dual exhausts. The car was lowered 2 inches in front, 3 inches in rear, with shaved doors, nosed and decked, rounded horn corners, 1956 Ford Victoria headlights, frenched 1951 Olds taillights, 1957 Olds parking lenses, tube grille, lakes pipes, moon discs, and bubble skirts."

"This photo of my 1959 Chevy El Camino was taken before any modifications. It was purchased when six months old. It had a 235 six-cylinder with three-speed manual transmission. The first modification was a split exhaust manifold with dual exhausts exiting in front of the rear wheels. Later came a 283 V8. Body mods consisted of electric doors, 1956 Buick portholes in hood holding buttons for doors, tonneau cover, 1959 Cad taillights with flat lens, Pontiac Bonneville seat, chrome interior moldings, and wheel treatment."

CHAPTER THIRTY-EIGHT:

MY 1964 CORVAIR MONZA SPYDER By *Mike Thibodeau*
EDITOR, LEAMINGTON POST

Several years ago I was watching a television program that featured a car buff simply wandering through an auto junkyard. He commented on various wrecks and rusted hulks and then stopped at a 1964 Corvair Monza Spyder that had seen better days. But his comment about the car focused on the dash, calling it one of the most unique and best instrument layouts ever designed. Yes ... a viewpoint I reached thirty years ago was finally supported by someone else.

After I married in 1968, my 1962 MGA no longer served as a family car, but a 1964 Spyder I spotted on a car lot in Pembroke would do nicely. I bought it and never regretted it.

The two main gauges, a tach and speedometer, were surrounded by smaller oil pressure, turbo boost pressure, cylinder head temperature, and generator gauges.

Driving in those eastern Ontario winters, the Spyder was perfect with its four-speed manual. The rear engine provided the perfect weight for traction. And just as vital, the air-cooled engine heated rapidly, sending warm air into the passenger compartment through vents under the rear seat.

The Spyder was sporty and would fly, not off the line, but up through second, third, and fourth gears. As the boost pressure rose the turbo started to give off a low-pitched howl with the rising RPMs.

Ralph Nader killed GM's Corvair, but over the years I have concluded that it was a vehicle suited almost perfectly for winter conditions in most of Canada, then and today.

CHAPTER THIRTY-NINE:

DUKE DEADMAN REMEMBERS HIS 1941 FORD CONVERTIBLE

This incredibly cool 1941 Ford ragtop was photographed by Duke Deadman at Jepson's Esso service station at Jones and Danforth in Toronto's east end in the spring or summer of 1957. The camera is looking north, the station is facing south, and the car is facing west. The owner (a fellow named Chuck) is behind the wheel. Soon after taking this photo, Duke bought the car. Chuck had just bought a house, and the car had to go.

Note the twin foglights, twin spotlights, fender-mounted radio aerial, wide white-walls, full wheel discs, shaved side trim, fender skirts, and chrome tailpipe extensions. The car appears to be lowered in the rear for that "speedboat" look so popular back then. A very cool photo of a very cool car.

Now let's roll the clock back an extra two years to 1955, when a young fellow named John Lewis was twelve years old. That's when John saw the car that got him hooked on old cars for the rest of his life. It happened at Bob Atkins' Esso station at Larchmount and Queen. This was a large station with a four-bay garage, and it was very close to where John lived.

A young man in his early twenties worked there. His name was Charlie Spencer, and he owned a rare and absolutely beautiful 1941 Ford convertible. It had just come back from a body shop when John first saw it: "You could smell the paint, it was so fresh!"

Charlie's 1941 ragtop sported a dazzling red finish, molded fenders, whitewall tires, fender skirts, chrome tailpipe extensions, and chrome air cleaners on the dual carb flathead V8 engine.

John volunteered to wash the car at the station for Charlie, and he did so several times. Charlie showed his appreciation by taking young John around the block in that fabulous car. He also took John, on numerous occasions, to the stock car races at the CNE on Friday nights.

Exposure to all this automotive excitement before he was even old enough to get his driver's licence made John Lewis determined to buy a car of his own — and that's what he did in 1957, when he was only fourteen.

For $60, he bought a 1941 Mercury convertible from Frank Lynch on Pape Avenue. The car was actually running with a rebuilt flathead under the hood. All the top fabric was gone, but all the top bows were still there. The car had an original radio with a button on the floor for changing stations. It still had its original brown leather upholstery, although by now all the seams were ripped. And it still had its original dark green metallic finish.

John later sold his 1941 Merc ragtop to Gerald Wagg, but he never took a photo of it. And he never took a photo of Charlie Spencer's dazzling 1941 Ford convertible.

Now fast-forward to March 2004, when veteran hot rodder Duke Deadman mailed a collection of his old car photos to yours truly, the Old Car Detective. Among the photos was the 1941 Ford convertible seen here at Jepson's Esso in 1957 with a fellow named Chuck behind the wheel.

Almost certainly, Chuck is the same Charlie Spencer who owned this car while working at Bob Atkins' Esso station two years earlier. And the car is almost certainly the same car that John Lewis fell in love with. That car was red, and the one shown here was red too. And after a lapse of forty-nine years, John Lewis can look at the car once again, thanks to the photo taken by Duke.

And what became of the car itself? Duke sold the car in 1958 to a fellow in Port Union, just east of Toronto. He saw the car once sitting in front of that fellow's house, then never saw it again.

1941 FORD
Series—Special, DeLuxe and Super DeLuxe

Serials not available.
(Located on left hand frame side member near steering column)
MOTOR—V-8. Precision-set non adjustable valve clearances. Dual down-draft carburetion. Automatic spark control, aluminum alloy pistons. Cast iron heads on Special, aluminum heads on DeLuxe. Develops 85 horsepower at 3800 R.P.M. B. & S. 3 1/16" x. 3¾". N.A.C.C. H.r. 30. P. Disp. 221 cu. in.
WHEELBASE—114". OVERALL LENGTH— 194 11/32". TIRES—6.00 x 16.
CAPACITY—Rad. 5 gals. Engine 4 1/6 qts. Gas. 12½ gals.
BRAKES—Hydraulic. Parking brake, mechanical at rear wheels.
BODY—All-steel, welded into one unit. Fully insulated. DeLuxe Models have following additional equipment. Dual Tail Lights and sun visors, wheel bands, robe cord (4 door sedans). DeLuxe instrument panel, Cigar lighter, Airfoam cushions, dual horns.
FEATURES—Balanced transverse springs. Torsional bar ride-stabilizer. X-type frame. Box section at points of greatest stress. Sealed Beam head-lamps. Steering column gearshift. Dual bottom mounted wipers clear windshield directly in line of vision. **Manufacturer's Outstanding Selling Features:** 1. V-8 Engine for smoothness, power and economy. 2. Triple-cushioned comfort. 3. Finger-tip Gearshift. 4. Battery Condition Indicator.

PASS.	MODEL	Weight Special DeLuxe	Super DeLuxe	Factory Retail—Windsor Special DeLuxe	Super DeLuxe
3	Coupe			$1080	
6	Tudor Sedan			1142	
6	Fordor Sedan			1205	
3	Coupe	2953		$1124	
5	Coupe A/S	2981		1167	
6	Tudor Sedan	3095		1186	
6	Fordor Sedan	3121		1249	
—	Station Wagon	3412		1462	
3	Coupe		2969		$1180
5	Cpe. (Aux. Seat)		3001		1224
6	Tudor Sedan		3110		1242
6	Sedan Coupe		3052		1292
6	Fordor Sedan		3146		1305
6	Con. Club Coupe		3187		1423
—	Station Wagon		3419		1544

All Prices License Extra

(96)

The 1942 Used Car Sales Handbook of Features was published by General Motors of Canada and gives data on all North American cars from Auburn to Willys between 1935 and 1941. The six-passenger 1941 Ford convertible weighed 3,187 pounds with a Windsor factory retail price of $1,423.

CHAPTER FORTY:

THE FIRST CAR BILL OTTON DROVE

Dorothy Pearsall of Leamington, Ontario, is married to Spencer Pearsall, a retired lawyer. Dorothy's maiden name was Otton, and she grew up with her four brothers, Doug, Bill, Bob, and Paul.

Four of the Otton children are in this photo: Doug (born in 1918) behind the wheel, Dorothy (1921) beside him, with Bill (1923) and Bob (1927) in the rumble seat. The photo was taken in the summer of 1937 in the Otton driveway at their home at 39 Elliott Street (four houses north of the Catholic church). The car is a 1930 or '31 Model A Ford roadster.

Bill began driving that summer, when he was fourteen. He was somewhat nervous at first, and because he wanted to avoid smashing into oncoming cars, he only did right turns as a novice driver.

Every Sunday, he drove his grandmother, Rachel Walker Otton, to St. John's Anglican Church, where she had her own pew. They headed north on Elliott, turned right onto Clark Street, stopped to let Grandmother off at the church, then south on Erie, another right turn, now heading west on John Street back to Elliott, with another right turn to get back home, where he turned right into the family driveway.

CHAPTER FORTY-ONE:

KEM JONES' 1936 FORD PHAETON

Kem Jones was born in Kingston, Ontario, on May 6, 1943. In around 1946, the family moved to Ottawa, where Kem grew up. To further his education, his parents sent him to High Mowing School, a Waldorf school in Wilton, New Hampshire, which he attended from 1959 to 1961. This school emphasized the student's creative development as well as academic growth.

Kem had a very strong interest in mechanics and began working in the school garage (Pagan Motors) learning the basics of car repair. He also got a volunteer job at Ken Blanchard Auto Salvage. The scrapyard dated back to the 1940s, and it was a good three-mile walk through the hilly New England countryside to the yard.

From one of his classmates, Sue Sessions, he heard about a 1936 Ford phaeton that had been sitting in her uncle's garage since 1954. With Kem's promise not to sell the car, Sue arranged for him to buy it for $50.

Kem's 1939 Ford Deluxe coach was his year-round car, and that included winter driving. Something under the hood is about to be checked while Kem's mother stands by.

This car became Kem's project for the fall of his senior year. Not only did he have to bring the car back to life, he also had to deal with all the paperwork required to bring the car into Canada. The car became mobile just before the end of the fall term. After driving it around the school campus a couple of times, Kem was confident enough to drive the

360 miles to Ottawa with his two buddies, Frank Mandy and John Radcliff. Someone forgot to tell Kem that he was running right into a blizzard. After two days of driving and numerous adventures, he made it home.

Kem crossed the border at 3:00 a.m. The customs officer was not interested in dealing with a kid with a clunker at that hour of the night, so he was told to keep going and to deal with the customs office in Ottawa. Kem attended the customs office on the afternoon of December 24, armed with the minor clause in the Customs Act that allowed all vehicles over twenty-five years old into Canada as general antiques. He also had the original 1936 list price of $590. Kem ended up paying $10 to some very relaxed Customs officers, as it was Christmas Eve.

With the car now in Ottawa, Kem kept working on it, at first in the backyard — but he really needed a garage. Being an enterprising young man with not much money, he made an arrangement with a senior widow down the street. He would look after her snow removal if he could use her vacant garage in the back lane, which had the classy name of Tackaberry Lane. Kem couldn't afford a guard dog, but he did install a seven-foot luminous skeleton on the inside of the garage door. When he worked late at night with the door open, this glowing skeleton could be seen in the dark. This may explain the local legend that the lane was haunted.

Kem's mother was very tolerant of his numerous late nights from working on the car. Often he would find his supper waiting on the kitchen table with strict instructions: "Don't go anywhere until you get rid of those smelly clothes and grease."

Kem describes his first restoration as strictly an amateur one based on what he knew at the time. He welded the weak body, frame, and running boards all together (creating perhaps the first uni-body 1936 Ford). Thin copper tubing was welded to the fenders to simulate fender welting.

Kem soon realized that a touring car with only flimsy side curtains and no wind-up windows was not a practical car for long, cold Ottawa winters. He located an unmolested 1939 Ford Deluxe coach on a gas station lot minus a carburetor for the astronomical sum of $600. Finally, after a lot of negotiation, Kem bought the car for $200. David, his brother, assisted with the finances with the stipulation that he got to use the car on some weekends. The 1936 Ford donated the carburetor from its flathead V8 engine to get the 1939 running. Kem drove the 1939 nearly every day until 1973, when he sold it for $500. It took him everywhere, even to a teaching position in Atikokan, Ontario (west of Thunder Bay).

Now back to the 1936 Ford. The car was first painted battleship grey. In 1964, Kem attempted a major restoration, finishing the car in 1966. Now black, it was used for a honeymoon trip to California that summer. The car was later repainted again, this time in tan with brown fenders.

In the late 1960s, Kem also acquired the remains of a 1939 Mercury convertible. This car had the luxury of roll-up windows. Under restoration for the last forty years, the car is now nearing completion in Kem's garage in Mississauga, Ontario.

The 1936 Ford would have required a tremendous amount of work to improve it, and so in the 1970s it was sold through Keith Acres at his auto museum near Cornwall, Ontario. The 1936 Ford phaeton went to someone in eastern Ontario, and Kem eventually lost track of it.

Kem's 1936 Ford was not his first car, although it was the first car he drove on the road. His first car was a 1946 Austin purchased for $40 in Ottawa in 1957 and later sold for $20. His dad was away for the summer and wanted his fourteen-year-old son to be kept busy taking a car apart. Kem enjoyed walking around with the keys of the car hanging out of his pants pocket. When the car was sold, he retained the leather front bucket seat. This seat now rests in his basement rec room.

Kem recently acquired a 1964 Mercury Comet convertible to go along with his 1939 Mercury convertible. He reflects that the 1964 Comet does not seem old to him, yet it is close to twice as old as the 1936 Ford was when he first bought it.

Kem Jones and three of his friends pose for the camera in Ottawa in August 1962 before leaving for a camping holiday in New England in Kem's 1936 Ford phaeton. Kem is standing by the driver's door. Note the stick-on tinted strip across the top of the windshield, a popular add-on back then.

CHAPTER FORTY-TWO:

BYRON WARWICK'S FIRST "CAR" WAS A TRUCK

Byron posed with his truck on Oak Street East in Leamington in July 1957, when he worked for the H.J. Heinz Company.

Byron Warwick was born on September 22, 1936, and grew up around Leamington, Ontario. While in high school, he worked part-time in the tomato fields for spending money and he worked in the summer for the H.J. Heinz Company. He usually got to school and work by hitch-hiking along Highway 18 to Erie Street South.

One day in 1955 at that intersection, he saw a 1934 Ford pickup truck for sale at the Supertest gas station on the southeast corner. A local resident named Reimer Edsal had traded it in for a 1954 Ford station wagon. The asking price for the 1934 pickup was $200. It was in excellent original condition with its dark green finish and had been purchased new as a delivery truck for Duke and Ternan, a shop on the main street of town specializing in auto parts and accessories, appliances, and radios. The original engine had been replaced around 1947 with a rebuilt one, and that was still in the truck in 1955.

Byron had to have it. He bought it and took it straightaway to Larry's body shop in Ruthven for a fifty-dollar repaint job in red with cream pinstriping and yellow spoke wheels. He also added a white tonneau cover on the pickup bed. The truck was a common sight around town in the late 1950s.

Byron worked in the lab at Heinz from 1956 to 1957, went back to school the following year, then moved to Sarnia in 1959 to work for Dow Chemical and then Esso. He was still driving his 1934 Ford pickup as regular transportation, and drove it home to

Leamington every weekend to visit his sweetheart, Barbara. They were married in 1960.

Seven years later, they purchased a beautiful home on the St. Clair River in Corunna (where they still live to this day). And the 1934 Ford pickup was still running when they moved in, with a 1954 Meteor flathead of 255 cubic inches under the hood. But time was taking its toll on the old truck, and the body was beginning to rust.

The original frame was badly rusted as well. A section of it actually broke, producing squeaks and rattles that prompted Byron to take his truck to a local mechanical shop, where a support piece was welded into place. He then drove the truck another two years before taking it off the road in 1968.

Byron's future wife, Barbara, posed on the hood in July 1957. They were married three years later.

But that wasn't the end of it. Byron *still* owns it fifty years after buying it! The truck went into storage for thirty-two years while Byron and Barbara raised their family and pursued other interests, including the building of bird houses (Byron has constructed approximately two thousand of them).

Then in around 1999, a friend phoned to say an old Ford truck was for sale on a street in Sarnia. Byron went to look at it. The truck was all in pieces and sitting on the ground. No engine and no wheels, but a 1934 Ford cab was sitting on a 1934 Ford frame with pickup box and rear fenders from a Model A, and front fenders from a 1932 Ford. Other parts included an extra 1934 cab (with only one door from the two cabs), a 1934 Ford grille shell, and 1934 Ford front fenders. Byron bought everything, then sold everything except the 1934 frame, 1934 front fenders, and spare grille shell.

The fellow who owned all this had had these parts for seven years, intending to build a street rod. Then he bought a house to raise a family, and the parts had to go.

Now Byron had a solid 1934 frame, and in the year 2000, he began taking his truck apart for a full body-off restoration. At the time of this writing (January 2005), he has a fully restored and running chassis, with the 1954 Meteor flathead V8 totally rebuilt and hooked up to the original transmission and rear end. Body work, paint, and interior are still to be done.

Two other collector vehicles are in the family. Byron and Barb have the last car owned by her dad (the late Mourice Mann), a low-mileage 1969 Chevelle two-door hardtop in excellent original condition.

They also own a fully restored red 1954 MG-TF sports car, which they acquired in 1995. It is identical (even to the colour) to a car purchased by Byron in 1959. When he and Barb were married in 1960, they drove in that car around Lake Erie on their honeymoon.

It was later sold and they lost track of it until 2003, when they found it again. It's in Smithville, Ontario, all in pieces but slated for a full restoration. Another story for another book …

CHAPTER FORTY-THREE:

MY UNFORGETTABLE TRIUMPH GT6 *By Kathy Vance*

I was in my twenties, it was the 1970s, and together I, my Irish Setter, and this car made it through a personal relationship ending to a new beginning. When I bought this car I didn't know who I was and who I should be involved with, and by the time I sold this car I was on the road to a solid life.

My friend John Hallum brought me to his New Edinburgh garage in Ottawa, where he was storing an old car for a friend of a friend, in the hopes that maybe I'd buy this old car that had no tires, wouldn't start, had rusted, and was taking up space.

Kathy Vance is facing south, the car is facing west, and the camera is facing north at the northeast corner of Roseberry Avenue and Banks Street in Ottawa. This car looks like it's going 90 miles per hour even when it's standing still.

The open door cast the only light on this forgotten beauty. I lost my heart, my breath, and in that instant my friends and family thought I had lost my mind. I bought it and thought, *Somebody like me, a.k.a. "loser," doesn't deserve something like this, a.k.a. "beautiful."* We would become a confident match, but clueless, and with little money, how could I rely on the kindness of strangers and friends?

Kevin McNevin became my friend and taught me how to balance the Triumph's dual carburetors and how to pop rivet a new floor so my feet would stay dry when it rained. I was so focused on getting it started and keeping it going that my friend Isamu Ono taught me the most important life lesson: that brakes and stopping come first in the hierarchy of things. Basic life lessons learned.

It's a head-turning kind of car. John was shocked that I looked nothing like the sexy babes in the TV commercials showing women in coveralls when I emerged all greasy from under the car. I was shocked that TV perception was so distorted from reality. While Kevin and I worked on the transmission, we sorted out life truths too, that although I would never stand a chance at a mechanic's job, neither would he, as a big, burly guy, stand half a chance as somebody's secretary.

A full racing harness to strap me in relaxed my mother's worries marginally and impressed a border guard, whose reaction was "somebody must really care about you." I drove all along the Eastern Seaboard, throughout Quebec, Gaspe, and camping in P.E.I.

One time at a campground at Lake George, New York, I was the only single woman tenting amongst all these caravan houses on wheels — "You must be a Canadian" — and dwarfed by the giants. Me and mighty wheels rolled on. Me, the Setter, and the Triumph had lots of energy, loved the lift-off of life, and ranged in search of adventures. Thrilled by the power, I learned to "listen" to the road and the engine and to appreciate the teamwork with guys who were just as crazy about this car as I was. Mistakes, yes, but falling asleep at the wheel of life was not one of them.

Known affectionately by some as my future coffin on wheels, the car, by sitting so close to the road, had a reputation for possibly bursting into flames when hitting a bump or dip in the road, thus igniting the gas tank. Spinning around was also a problem with this big-engine scooter. One fine autumn day driving westbound on the Ottawa River Parkway onto Parkdale, the car held the tight curve until it did a 360-degree turn, then just kept completing the curve. Reflexes and luck, adding up the odds-on favourite. I decided to sell after several exhilarating years of driving, caring, and sharing.

Isamu knew a fellow mechanic who was looking for a fast car. It was hard for us to get it across to the mechanic, who wanted the car, that it was tricky keeping it on the road mechanically, electrically, balancing the carbs — and its road handling (sliding, pitching, lifting, and spinning).

He bought it. And he gave me that look that says, "I'm a big guy mechanic, and if a little gal like you could keep it on the road, then I can with no problem." All that was missing was the pat on the head.

Isamu told me three months later the car was a lawn ornament in his co-worker's backyard. I was lucky. It had been his folly as it had been mine. I've never learned more about life from a car before or since. It brought me close to car fans, mechanics, friends, and family, providing a structure that has kept me awake in life and love — thrilled. Now when I think of balancing carbs, it's a whole other thing.

CHAPTER FORTY-FOUR:

BILL MYERS REMEMBERS ONE OLD CAR AFTER ANOTHER

Bill Myers was born in Toronto on Saturday, November 20, 1937, the day of the Santa Claus parade. When Bill was two years old, his dad bought a new 1939 Chevrolet coach from Toronto Motor Car Co. at Church and Lombard in downtown Toronto. A year later, the dealership had switched from GM to Ford, and Bill's dad bought a new 1940 Ford coach — a car that was later driven by the family on a holiday to California.

In 1947, Bill's dad bought a new Mercury 114 coach, again from Toronto Motor Car Co. This car was light grey, but it didn't stay that way. It was given a repaint job at Poole Motors in Bobcaygeon during a family holiday at Bill's brother's cottage. Now it was dark grey ("a very sharp colour," recalls Bill).

Bill's dad was Barry Myers. For fifty years he worked for Autographic Business Forms (known today as Autographic Business Machines). The company occupied the Lumsden Building near Adelaide and Victoria — and one of their customers was Toronto Motor Car Co. Ltd. at Adelaide and Church.

On a visit to Fawcett Motors in Whitby, Ontario, Bill Myers poses with pride alongside this fully restored 1935 Ford coupe with grey finish and red spoke wheels. This car brought back many pleasant memories of the one-owner 1935 Ford coach that Bill purchased for $150 from Toronto Motor Car Ltd. in September 1955.

That dealership advertised itself in the mid-1950s as "Canada's largest Mercury-Lincoln-Meteor dealer" and at that time had over two hundred employees.

Also at Fawcett Motors was this 1936 Ford four-door sedan needing a lot of work. The body shell is identical to Bill's 1935 Ford, which he bought in 1955 and sold in 1957. He is pointing to the place on the firewall where he drilled holes to install a heater in his 1935 Ford fifty years ago.

Barry Myers arranged for his son to land a job at Toronto Motor Car in April 1955 — and Bill began as a car jockey working five and a half days a week for $30 a week. The place was full of cars by eight o'clock every morning, and Bill drove "hundreds of cars every day" up and down the ramps of the five-storey building. The paint shop was on the top floor, the body shop on the third floor, and general mechanical repairs on the second floor. Many vehicles were stored in the building as well, including hearses and ambulances.

Soon after starting there, Bill spotted a dark blue 1939 Studebaker Champion coupe on the back row of the used car lot. It had belonged to a customer who had brought it in for some body work (rust was coming through). When the bill reached $500, the owner walked away from the car, and that's how it ended up in a back corner for sale.

Bill bought it for $50, thereby getting $450 worth of body work for nothing. There was no safety check, no PST, no GST, and the cost of transferring the ownership was included in the price. Dick Gardner, the service manager, handled the sale, and he personally stood and watched while Bill signed all the papers for the car. He was happy to get rid of it.

The fenders had been leaded in, and a friend said, "If the car ever breaks down, you can sell it for its weight in lead." The gas gauge didn't work, and the interior was filled

with dust from the body shop. Bill checked the gas by snaking a garden hose into the tank. He gradually got rid of the dust because his passengers had it all over their clothes every time they climbed out of the car. There was no radio, but Bill and his pals got around this by singing.

Bill's Studebaker did have two interesting features: electric wipers (when most cars had vacuum wipers) and "hill-holding" brakes. These brakes were first introduced on Studebakers in 1936 and consisted of a coupling between the clutch and brake to prevent the car from rolling backwards down a hill when the driver took his foot off the brake to step on the gas.

Bill finally sold the car, still running, for five dollars to Joe Smith, a tow truck driver at Toronto Motor Car Co. What became of it after that is a mystery.

One of Bill's co-workers at Toronto Motor Car drove a 1938 Plymouth with a rusty gas tank. He couldn't afford to have it fixed, so he drained it, then mounted a watering can on the firewall and ran a gas line to the carburetor. This meant he had to stop at nearly every gas station to fill up the can — but that was cheaper than trying to repair or replace the gas tank.

Bill's next car (after the Studebaker) was a really nice car — a well cared for 1935 Ford coach traded in by the original owner for a new 1955 Meteor at Toronto Motor Car.

By this time, Bill had been given a raise of $5 a week. That raise, bringing him up to $35 for a five-and-a-half-day week, "put me over the hump where I could now buy that '35 Ford." Bill paid $150 for it on September 11, 1955. He was seventeen years old, and the car was twenty. The odometer read 79,002 miles. It was the last year that Ford had spoke wheels, and this car had the spare mounted on the back with a metal cover and a lock for the spare under the Ford insignia. "It was a very sharp car," recalls Bill.

He soon discovered it had a top speed of 87.1 miles per hour. He checked his fuel consumption and discovered he was getting a respectable 19.2 miles per gallon in the city and 23.8 on the highway.

To upgrade the car, Bill installed sealed-beam headlights and a 1939 Ford generator purchased from the big Canadian Tire store at Yonge and Church. Some Model T Ford parts were still being sold there at that time. Bill replaced the original in-dash radio (cables and all) with a more modern radio for $15 and gave the original one to Father Riley O'Leary, a priest at St. John's Roman Catholic Church on Kingston Road. Bill installed that radio in the good father's 1938 Chevy.

When winter set in, Bill realized his car had no heater, so he bought one from an auto wrecker, drilled some holes in the firewall, and mounted it under the dash. "It didn't do much good," Bill recalls, "but it made you feel better knowing it was there. I drove up to Uxbridge with a bunch of guys early one morning for a hockey practice. It was 5:00 a.m.

and all the windows frosted up. I cleared a little of the windshield with my thumb as I was driving."

After owning his 1935 Ford for one year and nine months, Bill finally traded it off for a 1949 Chevy four-door at a car lot in Stayner, Ontario (where Bill's brother lived at the time). This brings the story up to the summer of 1957. That 1949 Chevy was Bill's fourth car (his first being a 1936 Chevy with a bullet hole in the trunk lid — see page 92).

Car number five was a 1951 Buick sedan purchased from A.E. Brown Motors on Main Street north of Kingston Road. Bill never forgot that car — especially because of what happened one night in the Loblaws parking lot at Main Street and Kingston Road. A chain had been put across the exit before Bill had a chance to leave. Not wanting to leave his car there overnight, he drove out of the parking lot by bouncing over a concrete curb, which tore off the rusty saddle straps holding up his gas tank. Only the copper fuel line now connected it to the car, and Bill could hear the tank dragging along the pavement as he drove off down the street. He stopped and climbed out to check the damage. He took off his belt and slung it under the car to reattach the tank. Then he drove home. That belt was still holding up the gas tank when he sold the car several months later.

No collection of automotive memories from Bill Myers would be complete without telling what happened one day while Bill was a student at St. Michael's Catholic high school at St. Clair and Bathurst in Toronto:

"One of my friends' dad had a 1950 Nash Canadian Statesman. Every so often, my friend drove it to school and we'd get a ride home. One day he had to stay in after school, so a bunch of us climbed into the Nash and used some aluminum foil from a cigarette pack to hot-wire the ignition. The starter button was under the clutch.

"We got the car running, then three of us jumped into the back seat and, with ropes and broom handles and everything else, drove down St. Clair Avenue with nobody in the front seat! All by remote control. The car had a standard transmission, so the three of us operated the clutch, the brakes, and the accelerator. We had strings running over the sun visor for the gears. Talk about insanity! We got funny looks from other drivers — then we realized how crazy we were, so we jumped into the front seat and drove the car back to school."

CHAPTER FORTY-FIVE

MY FIRST TWO CARS By Alvin Shier

Alvin Shier is a regular columnist with Old Autos. *With his Canadian Pontiac Registry,*
Alvin now has on file over six hundred Pontiacs built in Canada since 1926.
Here in his own words is the story of his first two cars.

This story begins in the northern Alberta town of High Prairie — my hometown. In 1962 at the age of fifteen I lived with my grandmother. Her home was a stone's throw away from the West Prairie River, which served as the town's western border. I spent lots of time as a kid swimming and fooling around in this river.

Each spring, however, the West Prairie would threaten to flood the town, and it did just that on more than one occasion. The oxbows in the river were perfect locations for logs to jam up, causing a tremendous damming effect, which often led to flooding.

At some point in the 1950s, the town decided to straighten out the section of the river that ran through the town in an attempt to alleviate the annual threat of flooding. One of the problem oxbows happened to be at the end of the street we lived on. When the town set about correcting the river, they built a bank along the widest part of the oxbow, thus leaving a small body of captive water which became known locally as the dairy pond.

Subsequently, the town encouraged people to dispose of their dry garbage in this hole, and the local body shop took advantage of this. All the write-offs from Ed & Jack's Auto Body (right across the street from Granny's house) and derelict cars and trucks eventually ended up in the dairy pond. I spent lots of time down at the dairy pond skating in the winter, rafting in the summer, and picking through the old cars and trucks. Hanging out at the body shop and the dairy pond is likely where I first developed my love for the automobile. Many years later, collision repair would become my vocation.

One thing I'm certain about is that the pond is where my first "car" came from. Each day after school I'd wander over to see what had been dumped in. One day a friend and I hit pay dirt. New to the pile was a creation consisting of an Austin A-40 frame with the front half of a Model T touring body attached. I had seen this "hot rod" being driven in the east end of town, and now there it was in the dump and mine for the taking.

A neighbour, Mr. Brasarb, helped drag the beast out with his 1953 Ford sedan delivery, and finally there it was in my grandmother's driveway — my very own car. The thing I loved about that car was those inside lever-type door handles common on Model T–type cars in the 1920s. You just reached in and pulled back on the lever, which released the latch, and the door opened. As a kid I played with those doors, oiling the latches and hinges and making them open and close perfectly. I never did get the car running or drive it, but I spent hours sitting in it and pretending.

My fun came crashing to a grinding halt one day about a month after "taking delivery of my new car" when my uncle told me to get "this wreck" out of the yard. Looking back on it now it sure was a wreck, but it was also my first car.

And now for my first car that actually ran …

In 1966, shortly after graduation from high school that June, I took a job on a Government of Alberta road building project near Grand Prairie, Alberta. My Aunt Jo Ann and Uncle Ben, who resided a few hours away in High Prairie, drove up one Sunday to visit. Aunt Jo Anne took one look at the literature hanging around the bunk house and said something like, "We're going to help you get a job where you'll be around better people."

No rear bumper and no hubcaps, but the car actually ran — the first car Alvin Shier had on the road. The kids in the photo (Vincent Sales and Christine Sales) are Ben and Jo Ann's children, now all grown up. The car is gone, but the memories live on.

I thought that the guys I worked with were just the greatest — but two weeks later I quit the road building job and hitched a ride back to High Prairie, where Aunt Jo Ann had arranged a job interview with the manager of the local Government of Alberta Treasury Branch, Percy Smith.

I landed the job and began working there the first Monday in September 1966. Bank workers have never been known to make outrageous salaries, and I was no exception. My gross pay was $230, my net $175. I agreed to live with my aunt and uncle and their young family "until I got on my feet" financially, and Aunt Jo Ann asked for only $75 (I know that I drank at least $75 worth of milk each month).

I didn't have a car, and my uncle was determined to find me one (probably to keep me from borrowing his brand new 1966 Impala). As manager of the local Beaver Lumber store in town, he knew everyone. One of those people was a Mr. Spendiff, owner of a trucking company bearing his name — Spendiff Transport. In Spendiff's yard sat a 1953 Chevy four-door that hadn't moved in years. Uncle Ben asked "old man Spendiff" for the car, and he gave it to me.

We found tires for it and then dragged it the few blocks to Ben's place, where we (mostly he) got it running after about three evenings of tinkering. Many trips were made to the local GM dealer to pick up things like spark plugs, points, etc. I remember going over the interior with a fine-toothed comb, and it was just like new when I finished. The next thing I did was spray-paint black primer spots all over (see photo) to give it that "under restoration/hot rod" look.

I don't recall exactly, but I believe the car had only forty thousand miles on the clock when I became its second owner. The engine burned oil like crazy, probably the reason for its original decommissioning. Since the Model T body on the Austin frame never did run and I never did drive it, old man Spendiff's 1953 Chevy became the first car I actually had registered in my name and drove. Since then I have owned upwards of thirty Chevys and Pontiacs of that era.

My honeymoon car in the summer of 1968 was a baby blue primered 1953 Chevy two-door hardtop that was lowered. The stock six had a Fenton dual carb set-up (which was awful on fuel) and a homemade split manifold with dual pipes, which in turn were split at the back into four pipes.

I tore the exhaust system completely off the car while trying a shortcut (fifty miles of rain-soaked dirt road) from one major highway to another in northern Alberta on our honeymoon, but that is another story completely. Still married — same girl! Unbelievable!

CHAPTER FORTY-SIX:

PAUL CLANCY'S "ALARM CLOCK" METEOR

Paul Clancy's 1951 Meteor Victoria hardtop, photographed in front of the family home in Port Credit (now Mississauga), Ontario, in 1957. Note the white-on-black Ontario plate and the fender skirt that doesn't quite match the colour of the body.

It was two-tone green with spinner wheel covers, fender skirts, and cement blocks in the trunk to get the back end down low. Twelve-inch dual pipes stuck out past the rear bumper, and the engine rumbled and roared through Hollywood mufflers every time the driver stepped on the gas. It was Paul Clancy's 1951 Meteor Victoria two-door hardtop.

It wasn't his first car, but it was the first one he owned when he moved out of the family home in 1957 when he was eighteen.

Paul was born in 1939 and grew up with his three younger brothers (Peter, Ford, and Gord) in the family home at 1414 Lochlin Trail in Port Credit (now part of Mississauga). His first car, while he was still in high school, was a blue 1929 Chevrolet rumble seat coupe (first year for Chevy's new overhead-valve six). He drove it some, then it sat for a while in his parents' driveway until it was finally towed away to a wrecking yard.

His 1951 Meteor Victoria was a car that every young man would be proud to own. The original flathead V8 was still under the hood and the transmission was a three-speed column shift. Paul added a suicide knob to the steering wheel so he could turn corners with one arm around his girlfriend, Jackie. The car had a green interior with a push-button radio that Paul kept at 1050 CHUM to catch all the latest rock'n'roll hits. CHUM adopted twenty-four-hour rock'n'roll in May 1957.

Paul squealed his tires a lot, and he used the car as an alarm clock when he first moved out and lived on his own. Terrified of being late for work, he slept in his car every night while parked across the entrance to the employees' parking lot on Lakeshore Drive. He was awakened every morning by his fellow workers blowing their horns and yelling at him. He was never late for work.

Later on, he sold his 1951 Meteor to a fellow named Brian Wilson. But while he owned it, he carved his name and his girlfriend's name on the steering wheel: "Jackie and Paul." They later got married. The car is gone, but they still have each other.

Leamington Post & News, *Thursday, May 3, 1951.*

CHAPTER FORTY-SEVEN

DON BROWN'S FIRST MUSTANG

Don Brown ordered this 1964 ½ Mustang in October 1963, a full six months before these pony cars went on sale.

It wasn't his first car, but it was his first new car. And it was definitely his first Mustang, because he ordered it six months before the first Mustangs went on sale.

Don Brown of Leamington, Ontario, has enjoyed driving cars since he was a kid. Born on August 6, 1937, he grew up on the family farm just west of town. The first car

Don's wife-to-be posed on the front fender of his 1963 Corvair on the street in Detroit where she lived. Don traded in the Corvair when he took delivery of his new Mustang in May 1964.

he remembers riding in was Dad's eight-cylinder 1937 Olds four-door sedan. In 1947 the Olds was traded for a cream-coloured Kaiser at Johnny Freund's dealership at 4 Princess Street. It might have been the only Kaiser in town.

"That was the first car I took out and drove to the back of the farm," recalls Don. "I was ten years old and got the car keys and put a cushion on the seat and took off! They wondered where the car went. We had a long driveway back to the railroad tracks."

The Kaiser was traded in through Murray Myles' Mercury-Lincoln-Meteor dealership at the Leamington Fair for a blue 1949 Meteor two-door with sun visor, whitewalls, fender skirts, and a chrome grille guard.

That's the car Don drove to get his licence "on Chestnut Street at Askew. I don't know who the man was, but my dad knew him. I got my beginner's there when I was fourteen. That was the last year you could get it that young. I got my full licence shortly after my fifteenth birthday. I turned fifteen in August [1952] and I had my licence.

"But before that, I had driven my dad on his bachelor fishing trips in the spring up to the islands near Parry Sound when I was eleven or twelve, pulling a boat. They were having such a good time while I was driving,

Don bought this maroon and cream 1951 Buick Roadmaster two-door hardtop in Sault Ste. Marie in 1959 and sold it in Leamington, Ontario, in 1962. This photo was taken on White Street in Leamington. The car is gone, but the houses are still there.

they had no idea how fast we were going. In those days, you didn't see the police like you do now. Back home, I drove the Meteor lots of places, including the drive-in movies up in Windsor."

The Meteor was later traded in on the next family car — a 1953 Ford, cream and green, with Fordomatic transmission.

Don's first car was a black 1949 Ford two-door from Wigle Motors' used car lot. "I bought it around 1954 or 1955. The car had been smacked in the back left panel. It was just sitting there, and it was green at the time. It belonged to Freddy Harris, and he worked at Ford in Windsor, so it went back and forth to work every day. It had about one hundred thousand miles on it. It was well broken in. The dealer repaired the body damage and painted the car black for me. The price for the car: $600. Paul Wigle was the salesman who sold the car."

Don landed his first radio job at CJCS in Stratford in 1956. He went there without his 1949 Ford because the engine blew "from old age," so he left it at the family farm. One night when Don was on the air in Stratford, a former teacher of his in Leamington, who was now teaching in Stratford, phoned the station to say hello.

Don's 1949 Ford engine was sent up to Windsor while he was in Stratford. It was rebuilt and hopped up at the same time, bored and stroked. "They did everything to it. I could take it from first to second at about sixty-five, and it would hit around ninety-eight in second, and when I dropped it into third, it went right past the top end."

He managed to beat a 1955 Buick convertible from Ohio late one night on Highway 11. "We got side by side and he thought he was beating me, but I was still in second gear. Then I dropped it into third and left him behind."

In March 1957 Don went to radio station CFCH in North Bay, where he remained with his 1949 Ford for the next two years.

In the spring of 1959, Don joined CBE Radio in Windsor as operator and producer. By this time the 1949 Ford "had died a natural death," and Don did without a car during the summer in Windsor.

In September 1959 he was on the move again, this time to radio station CJCS in Sault Ste. Marie, Ontario, where he was on the air as a deejay. While in "the Soo" he purchased a very nice 1951 Buick Roadmaster two-door hardtop — maroon with a cream top and whitewall tires. "I drove it home to Leamington for Christmas 1959, and the 'Dynaflush' [a nickname for Dynaflow] transmission started giving out somewhere between Mackinac and Port Huron. I managed to reach home and parked it in the garage at my grandmother's house at 13 Russell Street and left it there."

The Buick sat in Don's grandmother's garage for more than a year: "I moved back to Leamington around March 1961, started working part-time at CJSP Radio in April, and full-time in May. Then I called Charlie Banyai for a transmission job. He and his kids came down and got the Buick out of the garage. It had never been touched. They put the jumper cables on it, it turned over once, and it started. They took it to their shop and put a transmission in it. That cost me $100 in those days, and I never had a minute of trouble with the car after that."

Don drove that Buick until the summer of 1962, when he sold it to Bob Willan at CJSP for $500.

His next car was even fancier: a white 1955 Cadillac convertible with blue leather interior and a blue top. It was a private sale for $1,300 from the original owner on Riverside Drive in Windsor. It's one of the few cars Don owned that he never photographed.

He doesn't recall the name of the owner. He heard about it through a friend of his dad and bought it in June 1962. "It sure was a nice car," Don recalls.

The only repair it needed was the water pump, which gave out while Don was driving up north to Magnetawan. It was replaced at Addison Cadillac at 832 Bay Street in downtown Toronto.

Don can't recall who bought the 1955 Cadillac from him, but he clearly recalls his next car: a white 1963 Corvair four-door sedan purchased from Lou Tomasi at CJSP in Leamington. It was a stick shift, and Don recalls, "The little sucker would go pretty good."

Don Brown's grandfather's brother was Art Brown. He was photographed on a visit to California on August 13, 1940. The car is a 1939 Chrysler coupe.

It was a reliable car. The fan belt broke one day on Highway 2 as he was coming into Chatham — and that was the only repair the car needed while Don owned it.

His next car was brand new, and he ordered it six months before it was in production. "I ordered a new Mustang in October 1963 from Lyle Stacey Ford in Chatham. He was a client of mine, and I had seen an artist's rendition of the Mustang in *Time* magazine in August or September, and they had approximate prices. So I was in to see Lyle one day on business and I said, 'By the way, do you want to get me one of those Mustangs?' And he said, 'Well, we don't know how much they're going to be.' And I said, 'That doesn't make any difference. Just deliver it.' So he did.

"I was getting married on May 23, 1964, and the car arrived on May 19. It was the first Mustang in Leamington [they went on sale across North America just one month earlier]. There weren't even many in Miami when I got mine. Mine was white with a red interior. I drove it on our honeymoon and I drove it around town while I was working at CJSP Radio."

Don drove his Mustang for a couple of years, then traded it off for a new 1966 Buick Wildcat.

Other exciting cars followed as the years rolled by, including a mint 1968 Buick Electra 225, a 1967 Thunderbird, a 1971 Cadillac, and more Mustangs.

But nothing can take the place of the memories of his first Mustang — and his very first car, the 1949 Ford purchased while Don was still a teenager. The cars are gone, but the memories live on.

CHAPTER FORTY-EIGHT

IVOR PASCOE'S 1956 MONARCH

At age fourteen, Ivor Pascoe was working in a coal mine in his native Wales. Seeing a better life for himself in Canada, he crossed the ocean as a young man and never looked back.

In the 1930s he drove trucks for the Dufferin Coal and Coke Co., back when the hundred-pound burlap bags of coal were carried by hand from the truck to private houses. During the Second World War, he enlisted and served with the Royal Canadian Engineers' 18th Field Company, he participated in the early morning landing on D-Day, June 6, 1944, and he went with the Canadian Army through Holland and across the Rhine into Germany.

Ivor Pascoe's boss and best friend, Ezra Nash, always drove a late-model Cadillac, including the 1959 convertible shown here. Back then, these cars were huge boats with enormous fins that always caught the eyes of youngsters (and everyone else too!). Ezra loved gadgets and equipped his cars at various times with an early car phone, fridge, and coffee maker. Until late in life he was a highly respected business advisor, a great guy, and a real character. He is still fondly remembered by Ivor's son, Dennis Pascoe.

In 1945, Ivor was back in Toronto, and he resumed his previous employment with Nash Haulage. By the 1950s, he was the foreman and had the use of a delivery car for taking architectural and industrial blueprints to and from the Norman Wade Company. By the mid-1950s, his car was a light blue 1956 Monarch two-door hardtop with whitewall tires, full wheel discs, headlight eyebrows, a wraparound windshield, and lots of chrome. Ivor was very proud of this car, and he had his photo taken with it in front of the family home at 67 Kirknewton Road in July 1957.

The Monarch was available only in Canada, being the Canadian version of the Mercury. The Monarch was first introduced by Ford of Canada in 1946 to cash in on the pent-up demand for new cars at the end of the war in 1945 (no new cars for civilian use had been built since February 1942). The name "Monarch" was chosen because of the close ties forged between Canada and Britain during the war.

Ivor's Monarch was the tenth-anniversary model (although not designated as such) and might still be around today had it not been totally demolished in an accident on Roehampton Avenue in Toronto by another driver on delivery.

Not as flashy as the 1956 Monarch two-door hardtop, this silver 1961 Chevy was Ivor's company car in 1961, photographed that summer at Wasaga Beach, Ontario. Son Dennis remembers this car: "The bare-bones model. This side angle was best; rather ugly from the front, if you ask me. Dad would often let me drive his cars along the deserted hard-packed beach at Wasaga or on quiet country roads while I was much underage. These company cars were replaced every year or two."

CHAPTER FORTY-NINE:

THE FIRST CAR DENNIS PASCOE DROVE EVERYWHERE *By Dennis Pascoe*

It was a 1965 Envoy Epic (same as a Vauxhall Viva) — a General Motors economy car that rolled off the assembly line right in the middle of the tire-squealing, foot-stompin' muscle car era. The Envoy Epic could squeal its tires, but only if you drove around a corner on two wheels. As for horsepower, well, as my fellow Canadian automotive historian Gord Hazlett would say, "Not enough punch to pull the skin off a rice pudding." But Dennis Pascoe still fondly remembers his Envoy Epic.

Four on the floor and four-cylinder. An odd shade of red; I still had the tin of touch-up paint that came with it until recently. Apart from completely out-of-adjustment carburetor and timing when new, the car was pretty trouble-free once my dad [Ivor Pascoe] dealt with these problems. He was a motor mechanic and dispatch rider in the army, so he knew all about simple engines like this one.

Since the car my dad drove was supplied through his work, this was the only car owned by our family. It was essentially mine to drive to summer jobs at the Canadian Tire warehouse and around Toronto, especially on music gigs. During hot summer weather I would carry a thermos of ice water under the seat so I could have it on the long drive home from the warehouse. We installed a big old radio under the dash, which picked up all the noise from the ignition.

Since my dad's work car had to be available for work even when he was on his two-week holiday, this car was the family's vacation vehicle. It took us from coast to coast trouble-free. To the east coast in 1965, when this photo was taken in Fredericton, New Brunswick, and to the west in 1967. Our first time for both. Almost didn't make it up some very steep roads of those days in the Rockies.

It was sold to a fellow who moved with it out to Nova Scotia. He got an oil change one day, drove the car a few miles, and ground to a halt. The engine was dry. Some idiot had forgotten to fill up the engine with new oil, so the car was junked near the Canso Causeway in Nova Scotia. Too bad. It was a great little runabout, and I could afford the gas!

Four-year-old Dennis Pascoe was still in short pants when he sat on the running board of this five-window Chevy or GMC pickup truck in 1950.

Now ten years old and wearing long pants, Dennis is itching to slide behind the wheel of Dad's 1956 Ford and step on the gas!

CHAPTER FIFTY:
DAVID BOTTING'S 1936 McLAUGHLIN-BUICK ROADMASTER CONVERTIBLE SEDAN

In the 1970s, Dave Botting returned to Victoria, British Columbia, and photographed his car at Hatley Castle, where Eleanor and her mother, Laura, spent their last few months.

David Botting lives in Summerland, British Columbia. His 1936 McLaughlin-Buick Roadmaster convertible sedan was built by General Motors of Canada in Oshawa for a young woman in Victoria, British Columbia, named Eleanor Dunsmuir — and it was likely her very first car. Here now is the story of a magnificent Canadian-built automobile.

The Dunsmuir family of Victoria, British Columbia, ordered three 1936 McLaughlin-Buick phaetons for three of their daughters. They were on special order, and it took almost a year before they were delivered from Oshawa, Ontario, to Hatley Castle in Victoria.

Eleanor, one of the daughters, was not well at the time. She died in 1938 and never got to use her car. Alan Douglas Ford, a friend of the family, eventually bought the Phaeton that had been intended for her. He named the car Eleanor in her memory.

When David Botting was a young man in his twenties, he was quite familiar with the sight of Ford driving around in Eleanor and was impressed with the sight and power of the car. Because Ford was a friend of the Botting family, they would often socialize at various events. Botting recalls, "There was quite a group of us. We used to go out to Ford's home for dances where young men were in demand to dance with the ladies. Sometimes we would go to Sooke for picnics. After the picnic was over, A.D. Ford would wait until everyone had driven off. Then he would fire up this monster of a car and pass everyone on the winding island road.

"After Alyce and I were married, we moved to Manitoba. Later on, after the war, A.D. Ford wrote to me: 'They won't renew my licence, Dave. A car dealer wants to buy Eleanor and turn her into a taxi! If you want Eleanor, come and get her.'

"Alyce and I travelled by bus to Victoria. 'Now, Dave,' said A.D. when we arrived, 'the car is out in the heated garage. It's been checked over by the local garage man.'

"Because it was wintertime and the Canadian roads were terrible, we drove into the States. There was no effective heater in the car. When we found ourselves in snowstorms in North Dakota we discovered there were no defrosters either. We bought frost shields for the windows but they were no good in this weather. Eventually, at thirty below, the heavy oil in the motor prevented the car from starting. Instead of being towed, a truck pushed us into a garage where we changed to lighter oil.

"A.D. Ford had been concerned about the future of Eleanor. He had seen other car owners turn their vehicles into hot rods or worse. 'Promise me you won't make Eleanor into a truck,' he had said before we left Victoria in 1955. When many cars in Winnipeg had trouble starting, Eleanor would often go out in the snow and pull them until they started.

"The other two Dunsmuir cars did not survive as well as Eleanor. One car was wrecked by the Dunsmuir daughters. Its engine was taken out and used to run sawmill equipment. The rest of it ended up in a wrecking yard in Kamloops. It was purchased locally, restored, then sold to an American. The second car was last seen at Plimley's dealership in Victoria. Research has been done to locate these cars but they seem to have disappeared."

TRAVELS WITH ELEANOR *by Lois Dyck*

Eleanor has travelled thousands of miles across Canada and the States since leaving Victoria. She has travelled all the way, without car trouble, to Prince Edward Island. She arrived at the seventy-fifth Anniversary of the Buick Club of America in Flint, Michigan, in 1978. Of the six hundred Buicks assembled there, Eleanor attracted a lot of attention. She was put on display where reporters, impressed with this distinctive car, interviewed David. After he explained to them where British Columbia was located, he informed them about Sam McLaughlin's Canadian influence. The Bottings also travelled across the country to California.

In a recent letter to the Old Car Detective, Dave says: "I drive the car in the good weather and will give it to my son when I croak."

David Botting (right) has received many awards and trophies for displaying Eleanor at antique and classic car shows during the forty years he has owned the car. This photo was taken on April 15, 2000, at the Cherry Lane car show, where David's McLaughlin-Buick won the tropy for Best in Show.

CHAPTER FIFTY-ONE:

ALEXA DeWIEL REMEMBERS HER FIRST TWO VW BEETLES *By Alexa DeWiel*

My very first car was a brand new 1970 Volkswagen Beetle, which was unfortunately repossessed only three months after purchase when I left a good job as film librarian in the sparkling new Ontario Science Centre in Toronto to become a waitress/poet in a student diner. This career transition precluded my being able to keep up with my car payments. Off went Beetle number one with the repo man.

My real first car, then, was a used 1968 (I think) Beetle that I bought for about $50 and hand-painted with a floral design to cover its front end dents. The times were a-changin'. With friends, I was living on the outskirts of Toronto and harbouring draft dodgers and a Green Beret gone AWOL from the war in Vietnam. It was useful to have a set of wheels. My VW Beetle also enabled me to be actively involved in the People or Planes movement, which successfully agitated to prevent the expropriation of farmland for the construction of a proposed airport northeast of Toronto.

My Beetle carried me through a tumultuous winter, its heater never quite working to capacity — and of course, because of the flowers, drawing negative attention on Highway 401 during my infrequent trips into the city. But I loved the soft purr of its engine, the comfortable knob of its gearshift, and the fact that it didn't seem to mind the pot holes in the ludicrously long driveway of our rented farmhouse.

Then one autumn morning in 1972 it just wouldn't start, and we pushed it to the back of the barn. This Beetle's demise eventually convinced me to move back into the city, where streetcars operated night and day and a certain Datsun 510 was soon to appear in my future.

Alexa's second Beetle was photographed in 1972 with her behind the wheel and a Green Beret about to climb in. These cars symbolized the "flower-powered" counterculture of the 1960s.

CHAPTER FIFTY-TWO

DAVE McMURREN'S FIRST FEW CARS

Dave's loyalty to the Chrysler Corporation is legendary. His 1967 Chrysler 300 convertible looks and runs just like new.

Dave McMurren was born Friday, December 19, 1941, and has spent most of his life in Woodslee, a small town in southwestern Ontario. When he was seventeen, his brother Doug bought a 1940 Plymouth four-door sedan for $20, then gave it to Dave. It was in running condition, but not for long. Dave had just one drive with it, to Essex and back home. Just before reaching home, the engine blew a piston.

"You should have seen all the smoke," says Dave. The car sat in the yard at home for a while, then was scrapped.

His next car was a burgundy 1948 Plymouth four-door sedan bought around May 1, 1961, from Victor St. Pierre in Belle River for $125. It was a high-mileage car but in excellent condition, and it ran well. Dave drove it for about a year. Then one night in July 1962 the car caught fire while parked outside. He looked at it the next morning and realized it had to be scrapped.

Before this happened, he already had another car — a 1955 Buick Century hardtop. He bought it from a man in Blenheim, Ontario, for $125 in December 1961. It was light blue and it had a four-barrel carburato on the 322 cubic inch "nailhead" V8. One night,

Dave was driving along a gravel road at high speed with six people in the car. One of his front-seat passengers decided to snap the Dynaflow transmission into reverse! The car slid sideways till Dave got it back into drive. The car continued to go for a few more miles — then the transmission and rear end gave out. Dave replaced both units, but the car was never the same after that.

Meanwhile, a fellow in Woodslee owned a VW Karmann-Ghia. His name was Ray Diemer and he took Dave for a ride. Dave loved the look of the sporty Italian-designed body, and he loved the way it handled. He had to have one.

He found it in the spring of 1962 on a car lot in Windsor. It was a 1957 Karmann-Ghia hardtop, and Dave drove it off the lot for $1,200. It was red with a black top and had a four-speed floorshift. A friend rebuilt the four-cyclinder rear-mounted engine for Dave for $110. If you ran out of gas, you could flip a lever for a reserve tank with enough fuel to get you to a gas station.

His only complaint was the heater. It wasn't much good. But everything else about the car was great, and Dave drove it till 1966, when he traded it off on a car lot for a 1962 Valiant to make room for his growing family.

For the next twenty years, he drove family cars, but he never lost his interest in the older models. In 1987 he began looking for a Chrysler convertible from the 1960s and found the car he wanted

With hair that turned him into an Elvis look-alike, Dave drove this four-speed 1957 Karmann-Ghia from 1962 to 1966.

in Newmarket, Ontario: a 1967 Chrysler 300 convertible in excellent original condition. It has a beautiful Turban Bronze finish and all-white interior. Under the hood is a 440-cubic-inch V8 with a four-barrel that cranks out at least 350 horsepower. It was a rare car even when new, with only 1,594 convertibles produced in the 300 series.

Dave and his wife have driven their convertible to many cruise nights in their area and to car meets in Michigan, Dayton, Ohio, and Memphis.

Dave began working for the Chrysler Corporation in Windsor in 1963 and has remained loyal to that make ever since. In addition to their 1967 convertible, the McMurrens also drive a 2000 Dodge Grand Caravan, a 1999 Dodge Ram pickup, and a 1993 Dodge Spirit. Walter P. Chrysler would be proud!

Jack Bridgen owned this 1940 Chrysler convertible in Essex, Ontario, in the 1950s. It was built the same year Walter P. Chrysler died.

CHAPTER FIFTY-THREE

MY FIRST CAR — AN MG TF *By Bob Janzen*

The year was 1954. I was fifteen and had been smitten by the sports car bug. We lived in Caledonia, Ontario, on Number 6 Highway. On weekends we would sit on the front porch watching all the cars go by on their way to Port Dover or Turkey Point. There were some pretty nifty rigs cruising by, but to my mind's eyes and ears, the smaller, sleeker, louder ones excited my senses most. When an MG, Triumph, or Jaguar went by, I could hardly contain myself.

My dad was sympathetic to my reactions, as he had ridden motorcycles and hot rods for many years before. One day, he said, "Come on, Bob, we're going to the city today."

Hamilton was only twelve miles to the north. Back then Highway 6 was hilly, winding, and dangerous to the top of the mountain, and then came the descent around the hairpin curve to the city. It was a beautiful sports car road.

Bob Janzen's dream machine photographed fifty years ago: grey body, tan top, red leather seats, four-on-the-floor, wire wheels, cut-down suicide doors, and a rear-mounted spare. No wonder it was love at first sight.

We navigated our way to Gulliver Motors, a British car dealership in downtown Hamilton. It was late summer, and through the showroom windows we could see the Rovers, Hillmans, and TR-3s. Once inside, there were others, including MGs and Jaguars.

The new MGA had just been introduced. It looked great, but after so many years of seeing the sleek, sloping fenders and slab rear end with a spare on the back, it was hard to get used to this new rounded design. Dad and I still preferred the classical lines of the TC, TD, and TF.

We priced the MGA on the showroom floor. It was $2,395. The salesman extolled the features of the car and let us wander around. We were about to leave when he sensed that maybe we were in a buying mood. He said, "Come on out back. I might just have something you fellows would be interested in."

To the back we went, into the corner of the repair shop. He turned on the lights and there it was — an absolute classic beauty — waiting. The MGAs were so much more modern looking, but to me this MG TF was the epitome of sports car design. It was a beauty — grey with a red leather interior, tan top, wire wheels, one of the last TF MGs. Wow!

Even Dad got excited. I was glad, because he was the one who could make this dream come true. After haggling for quite some time, the salesman came up with a price that we all agreed on — $1,850.

The next day, we picked up the little MG after it had been checked over and licensed. Out the door and onto the street we went. After half a century, I can still smell the leather seats and hear the SU carbs doing their thing. Dad and I headed for the mountain and Caledonia. Hamilton Mountain looked formidable, and in those days and for a 50-horsepower MG, it was.

I rounded the hairpin curve, geared down to third, and gunned it. Wow! She was a real hill climber. We made it! We travelled the twelve miles to Caledonia in a state of ecstasy and arrived at Caledonia Tractor, an Allis Chalmers dealership that Dad owned.

The guys from the back shop came out to see this new gem. Some liked it a lot, while others claimed that they would rather stick to their Chevys and Fords. That is as it should be, but I was in love with my MG. The top was seldom raised, and cruising around Caledonia and the Grand River area was extremely pleasurable.

Later that year, Dad got a notice that Allis Chalmers needed a dealer in the Essex County area, so we moved to Kingsville and set up a dealership in Harrow. The MG also made the move. My sister Anita and I drove the MG to school at UMEI [United Mennonite Educational Institute] for about a year, after which time we decided that this car was impractical for our current needs.

I traded it at Wills Motors in Caledonia for a 1957 Chevy station wagon. The last I heard, the TF sounded much different from the original sound that I could remember. You see, John Wills had replaced the tiny four-cylinder engine with one of his Chevy V8s.

I have had a dozen or more sports cars over the years, but that little MG is unforgettable.

CHAPTER FIFTY FOUR:

ON THE ROAD TO A NEW LIFE: MY 1973 PONTIAC FIREBIRD ESPRIT

By Margaret Quick Baltzer

Suddenly single in 1972 after the death of my husband and high school sweetheart, I was thrown into a new life not of my choosing at twenty-two years of age. Even though I worked as a full-time legal secretary, I learned very quickly first hand the discrimination that existed at that time regarding women and financial matters. Banks at that time could refuse a loan or home mortgage based on accepting only one-third of a woman's wage because she might "start a family"! So, there I was with no credit rating and trying to make my way in this new life with roadblocks that today's young women would find unbelievable.

I set about buying a house and getting credit cards in *my* name, and thirty-three years later, even through remarriage, I am still fiercely protective of the credit rating I built in my own name.

With this in mind, in 1973 I decided that I would sell my late husband's 1971 Firebird and purchase my first car — a 1973 Firebird Esprit. Fortunately, my brother, Robert Quick, was an engineer with General Motors in Oshawa, and I was able to buy my Firebird through him (Robert will retire this year after forty years with General Motors as a Director of Advanced Vehicle Integration, North American Engineering).

Margaret Quick Baltzer perches on the front fender of her new 1973 Firebird Esprit at her home on Division Street South in Kingsville, Ontario.

I was "on the road" to my new life in my new 1973 Firebird Esprit that was "Florentine Red" with a (peculiar) orange stripe and a 350-cubic-inch American Pontiac engine turning out 150 horsepower. Air conditioning consisted of rolling down the windows, and I motored along listening to Elton John's 1973 hit "Goodbye Yellow Brick Road" on the radio — without cassette. In 1973 General Motors first offered a cassette player as an option, but very few people bought it, preferring to stay with their eight-track players!

Its Endura rubber nose had been strengthened to three inches thick with a steel reinforcement bar in order to meet the government's new five-mile-per-hour impact mandate and was the last year for it before changing to fibreglass.

In 1973 General Motors produced 46,313 Firebirds, of which 17,249 were Espirts, at its long-ago-closed Norwood, Ohio, plant. Firebird sales dropped by 50 percent in 1973 due to the gas crisis that saw gasoline go from 35 cents (U.S.) to 75 cents per gallon and higher insurance rates.

These were troubled times for all car manufacturers as well as General Motors. Rising gas prices, insurance, new government regulations, and labour issues — the 1973 Firebird body style was originally to be released in 1972, but a long GM strike delayed the launch — all this contributed to the market and global economy we have today.

CHAPTER FIFTY FIVE:

A DEALER'S SON REMEMBERS "MY LITTLE BUICK" By Jay Ardiel

It was the summer of 1967 when, at age seventeen, I got my driver's licence in Windsor in my mom's 1967 Firebird 326 convertible. I was a part-time lot attendant at H.D. Bryant Motors, a Pontiac-Buick dealership at Tecumseh and Parent in Windsor.

My dad, Bill Ardiel, was general manager of that dealership. He looked for a franchise for himself with Chrysler, Lincoln-Mercury, and of course GM for a full year in 1967 and early 1968. We travelled far and wide from our area to as far as Toronto to check out locations for a franchise.

We had meetings with Chrysler and Ford and GM on and off. I can remember a Chrysler Co. trip for Dad to take over Pajots Chrysler, a very small dealership in Amherstburg, but it didn't work out, even though some Road Runners and GTXs sat on the lot.

Then one day, Dad, myself, and my sister Julia took a trip to Leamington to look at a GM prospect for Dad. We drove into town from the north along Highway 77 with the 5th Ace motorcycle gang running on each side of us. My sister and I were terrified (nice welcome). Dad said, "It's okay, kids. I'll sell them cars and get them off those things."

We turned left onto Mill Street East and there it was — the Ray A. Young Pontiac-Buick-GMC dealership. Not much bigger than Pajots Chrysler, no stock, no Road Runners, and no GTX's. Boo-hoo! It was so old and grungy looking. Yuck!

We drove around and down Erie Street South (tree-lined then) and to the Point, then back and around Seacliff Park. Dad fell in love with Leamington. He knew this was the best place for his family and his business. He also knew that people like Ray A. Young and his staff were dedicated and hard-working. Well, to no surprise, Dad negotiated a deal with GM Canada and Ray A. Young. We were leaving Windsor.

I moved to Leamington in late 1968 to live with my dad at Wigle's Motel. My mother and sister joined us here in 1969 after our home in Windsor (Riverside) was sold. We all cried when we left that home for the last time.

At my dad's new Leamington dealership, I worked the gas pumps out on Mill Street, cleaned and prepared the dealership for its opening, made new friends, and grew up fast. The dealership was very family-oriented. Anything that needed to be done got done. I was so excited back then with a chance to be an auto mechanic apprentice.

Finally the 1970 Grand Opening of Bill Ardiel Motors Ltd. for Pontiac, Buick, and GMC trucks. We opened with great fanfare, dignitaries, GM people, and even old friends, including the Fees from Covington, Kentucky. (Chester was the police chief there and we had met them in Florida a few years earlier.) What a surprise for Dad when they pulled up on Mill Street that night!

I worked as a car jockey and grease and oil tech six days a week plus nights. I was treated the same as anyone else in the dealership and on a punch clock. Dad would not have it any other way, and I got myself into trouble just as fast and the same as any fellow employees.

Well, my hard work paid off, and I wanted, like any other young man, to have my own car. I approached my dad about him maybe giving me a car. My father said, "Absolutely not," as I was given demos all day and occasionally drove my dad's demo home. Also, my mom had a family car brought down from Windsor.

But I still wanted my own wheels. So Dad said, "Go to the bank. I'll give you a good price but you have to get a loan." I could only get $2,500 up front. I wanted a GTO so bad (dream on), but even then, insurance was horrendous for a young guy like me.

Our dealership became an instant success and deals were made very quickly and trade-ins were rolling in. My dad's parts manager, Jack Foster, and his wife, Vivian (who worked for Dad also), were just like parents to me. They were beautiful people and very hard-working. The parts department was the central heartbeat of our dealership.

Jack suggested to me, why didn't I buy a nice little used car to start off with, then as I got into my auto mechanic's apprenticeship, I could upgrade. Maybe I could buy a two-door sixties car coming in and build it up to my liking. It would be fun and would give me a chance to work on it and learn.

Just a few weeks later, Jack and Vivian told me that a good customer of Ray A. Young were trading in their mint 1967 Buick Skylark Custom two-door coupe. They were a business couple who owned the Vogue Beauty Salon in Leamington across from what is now the Village Inn Hotel on Erie Street South. I believe they were somehow related to Jack and Vivian.

They were trading up to a larger car, and so their Skylark came in as a trade-in in the early spring of 1971. It was a mint green coupe with white interior (not my favourite colour), but it was in immaculate shape. It had a 340-4 bbl. engine, power steering, power brakes, tilt wheel, AM-FM radio, no air, rear defroster, not loaded — but it had a beautiful shape, especially the "gull-wing" roof line so popular back then in the mid-size GM line.

After a trip to the bank manager, it became my first car. I was on cloud nine. It was the first time in my life I was approved for a loan, and I got a lot of car for $2,000.

Soon after that, I became tired of its plain look and ordered Cragar S/S wheels and bigger tires through Jack and Vivian, followed shortly by an under-the-dash eight-track stereo and four-speaker package with "Reverb" (wow!). I added Delco air shocks on the back and a Skylark GS dual exhaust system with chrome tailpipe tips.

Other than the colour, my car really rocked. It was a great style for GM, and the wheels and tires transformed it into a really nice cruising machine. The little Buick never skipped a beat. I think I washed and polished the finish off it, as Dad's wash-bay was always open to anyone.

The picture shown here is of me at age nineteen in front of our home on Kenyon Point Road in that summer of 1971. I had a small checkered flag with my racing helmet (for my moped) and me wearing new GM mechanic's coveralls.

My sister Julia took the picture (she didn't complain because her brother and the "little Buick" became her taxi). Parked close by was my dad's parts truck, a blue and white 1971 GMC 1500 High Sierra pickup with this caption on the side: "The Best Deal is Ardiel." I was so proud and happy for Dad and so happy to finally have my very own first set of wheels.

CHAPTER FIFTY-SIX:

A 1940 MERCURY IN MANITOBA By Paul Horch

The following letter arrived recently in the Old Car Detective's mailbox.

Dear Bill

Thanks for autographing your latest book for me (*60 Years Behind the Wheel*). I have been reading it every day since I got it. I love books like that, just real people with real everyday cars. I was born in 1947 and I am told that by the age of about two, I could tell the make of every car on the road. That's more than I can do with today's cars!

Rescued from years of neglect while parked in a field, Paul Horch's fifty-dollar 1940 Mercury looked like this when he drove it around his Winnipeg, Manitoba, neighbourhood in 1969 (thirty-six years ago!). Note the original Sahara Tan finish on the firewall and upper cowl.

As promised, I am sending you some pictures of my 1940 Mercury four-door, which I purchased November 11, 1968. An easy date to remember! I paid $50 for the car, and it was truly in bad shape. Generations of mice had made their homes in it for who knows how long, and the car was just generally neglected and had been sitting in the middle of a field for quite a while.

I brought it to my sister's place (now my house) and covered it with the remains of an old tarp. A pretty sorry sight, especially with all the snow. Over the winter I had the distributor rebuilt with hopes of getting the car running in the spring. Little did I know…. In spring, with the car not starting, I removed the engine and decided it needed to be rebuilt … needed replacing. The block was cracked!

I found an uncracked engine at Princess Auto in Winnipeg. They were still in the auto wrecking business then. I had the engine rebuilt, and by the fall of 1969 the car was running. It still looked pretty rough, and I can't believe I had the nerve to drive it around the neighbourhood like that! No licence or registration or insurance. I guess God looks out for fools and idiots!

The serial number of my car is 1D2. I contacted the late Herman Smith at Ford of Canada, and he confirmed that my car was the second Mercury off the Canadian assembly line for 1940. It was probably assembled in late 1939 as the remaining original glass is marked October 1939. This probably makes it the oldest running 1940 Canadian Mercury in captivity, unless someone saved number one for some reason.

By the spring of 1970, my car was licensed and insured and I was driving it around. The bumpers had been re-chromed. I think the cost was about $16 each. Times sure have changed, haven't they? I managed to purchase a set of new old stock running boards from a fellow in Montreal. They cost me $70 including shipping! Wasn't that a good time to be restoring an old car?

During the spring and summer of 1970, I stripped the car down to bare metal and turned it

It looked just as rough from the rear, with blotches of primer all over the body. No plates and no insurance, but Paul Horch couldn't resist taking it for a spin.

Hard to believe it's the same car! Paul snapped this photo of his 1940 Mercury in October 1987, next to a pair of Texaco clearvision gas pumps, still widely in use when this car was new. Paul used this photo for his 1987 Christmas cards.

over to a friend who worked in an auto body shop. He worked on the body in his off-hours. He did a great job on the body and even used some lead in some of the repaired areas. The car had almost no rust. Just two little holes on the front edge of the rear fenders where they meet the running boards.

The body work was done and the car was primed with zinc chromate and then red lead. The paint was done late in June, and on the first of July the car was reassembled and out on its first tour three days later. Paint and body work cost $300.

That first tour was a run out to Portage La Prairie, about sixty miles west of Winnipeg. Somewhere along the way, I put on a set of fake whitewalls. Better than nothing, I guess. Also in 1970 I installed fog lights. The upholstery still had not been redone. That was completed around 1972. And around 1974 I installed a new set of Denman wide whitewalls. That sure made the car look great.

By 1979, I had worked up the nerve to install a spotlight on the driver's side. It actually has a Mercury 8 emblem on the inside handle, but I don't know if it is genuine Ford or an aftermarket item. I never did connect it because at the time one needed a permit to use a spotlight.

By the early 1980s, I wasn't driving the car much because I always seemed to have overheating problems. Not just a little hot but excessively *hot*!!!

Finally, during the winter of 2002–2003 I removed the radiator and sent it in to be recored. The top tank was shot so a new one was built. They did a beautiful job, and I now have a five-core rad in the car. It has never overheated again, even when the temperature hit the high thirties. I also had a dual exhaust system installed. Sure sounds nice!

I hope you enjoy the pictures and the story of my 1940 Mercury. The car has now been a part of my life for over thirty-six years. I put over thirteen hundred trouble-free miles on it in the summer of 2003. It cruises easily at any legal highway speed and handles very well since I installed the missing sway bar two years ago.

Once again, I am really enjoying your latest book. Thanks again, Bill.

Paul A. Horch,
Winnipeg, Manitoba

1940 MERCURY

Serials—09A-101701 and up—Started Oct., 1939

(Located on left hand frame side member near steering column)

MOTOR—V-Eight. Aluminum heads. Non-adjustable precision set valve clearance. Dual downdraft carburetor. Automatic spark control. Aluminum alloy pistons. DEVELOPS 95 horsepower at 3100 R.P.M. B. & S. 3 $\frac{1}{16}$" x 3¾". N.A.C.C. H.P. 32.5. P. Disp. 239 cu. in.

WHEELBASE—117 inches.

OVERALL LENGTH—195¾ inches.

TIRES—6.00 x 16—4 ply. Pressure 30-30.

CAPACITY—Rad. 4½ gals. Engine 4 qts. Gas. 13 gals.

BRAKES—Hydraulic Lockheed. Parking brake, mechanical at rear wheels.

BODY—All steel, one unit. Friction type ventilators. Passengers cradled between wheels. Wide restful seats. Body fully insulated against cold, heat and noise. Doors stay open when opened.

FEATURES—**Balanced transverse springs.** Torsion bar ride stabilizer. **Sealed Beam headlamps.** DeLuxe two spoke steering wheel. **X member frame,** box section at points of greatest stress. **Manufacturer's Outstanding Selling Points:** 1. Triple-cushioned comfort. 2. Power and Economy. 3. Ford V-8 Engine.

PASS.	MODEL	WEIGHT	RETAIL FACTORY WINDSOR
5	Sedan Town 4 door	3090	$1228
5	Sedan 2 door	3005	1173
5	Sedan — Coupe	3080	1228
5	Coupe Club Convertible	3075	1343
6	Sedan Convertible	3250	1519

All Prices License Extra

"A Greater Mercury 8 Ready for More Records"

(192)

According to page 192 of the 1942 Used Car Sales Handbook of Features, published by GM of Canada, Paul Horch's 1940 Mercury four-door Town Sedan weighs 3,090 pounds and had a Windsor factory retail price of $1,228. The two-door sedan weighed 3,005 pounds, indicating that the extra two doors on the Town Sedan added an extra 85 pounds to the car's overall weight. Oddly enough, U.S. serial numbers are shown. Canadian serial numbers began with 1D1. Paul Horch's 1940 Mercury is 1D2.

CHAPTER FIFTY-SEVEN:

A 1949 CHEVROLET IN SASKATCHEWAN

Peter Lehn of Leamington, Ontario, recently passed along two interesting old photos to the Old Car Detective, one with a car, the other with a truck.

The car is a 1949 Chevrolet four-door sedan photographed around 1951 on Lakeshore Tree Farm near Saskatoon, Saskatchewan. It was owned (and purchased new) by George and Antonia Krahn, seen here with their three children, (left to right) Robert, Richard, and Jean. Despite having picked up some Saskatchewan mud, this battleship grey 1949 Chevy still looks good with its curved two-piece windshield, big outside sun visor, and sleek "fast-back" styling. GM built over 1 million Chevys for the 1949 model year, but still got beaten in the sales race that year by the also newly styled 1949 Ford, which had a head start by going on sale in June 1948.

The second photo shows a new 1950 Ford pickup truck on a farm near Leamington.

CHAPTER FIFTY EIGHT:

GEORGE AND KEITH QUICK IN PAPPY'S WRECKING YARD

It rolled off the assembly line just after the end of the Second World War — a gleaming black 1946 Chevrolet four-door sedan. The new owner must have been very proud.

Thirteen years later, this same 1946 Chevy roared up a ramp, sailed through the air, and T-boned another old car at the Leamington Fair in the summer of 1959. Then it was towed to Murray Quick's wrecking yard about two miles northwest of town, where it was photographed, then scrapped. This is the story of its final week as a car.

In 1949, Murray Quick started an auto wrecking business beside and behind his house at the intersection of the third concession and Albuna town line just west of Leamington. Now deceased, Murray was the proud father of five sons — Bob, Albert, George, Keith, and Virgil. Quick's Auto Wreckers is still going strong today with Ab running the business.

In 1959, Paul Riddell and the Hell Drivers dazzled a cheering crowd of spectators with thrills and spills and smash-ups in front of the grandstand at the Leamington fairgrounds. Two of those spectators were George Quick (age twelve) and Keith Quick (age seven). The two brothers saw the 1946 Chevy fly through the air and T-bone another car. The crowd went wild!

After the thrill show, the 1946 Chevy was towed to Murray Quick's wrecking yard. George tinkered with it and got it running and began driving it around the yard with his little brother Keith on the front seat beside him.

The oil pan was dented and punctured by the T-boning, and George and Keith had to keep adding oil as they drove the car around the yard. The crankshaft kept hitting the oil pan and made an awful racket!

Also, the fuel line was broken, and Keith had to hold on his lap a one-gallon jug of Heinz vinegar filled with gasoline and with a rubber hose connected to the fuel pump. Even though the windshield was missing, the exhaust fumes inside the car were so bad that Keith got a headache — but not before sticking his head through the windshield so his mother could snap the photo you see here while the engine was running. George's hands can be seen on the steering wheel.

Soon after the photo was taken, the car was scrapped. Keith remembers taking off the front fenders with an axe. The end of a fine old car.

Do we have any idea who owned this car before it fell into the hands of the Hell Drivers? There is one clue. Clearly visible on the roof as the car sailed through the air at the Leamington Fair were these words: "Hyatt — Try It and Buy It!" Hyatt Motors was the local Plymouth-Chrysler dealership at that time. Someone apparently traded in the 1946 Chevy at Hyatt's used car lot. That person might still be alive and might be reading this book. If that person's story comes to light, you'll read all about it in my next book of old car stories. Stay tuned!

CHAPTER FIFTY-NINE:

TIPS FROM THE OLD CAR DETECTIVE

Ever wonder what became of your first car, or your favourite car? Was it scrapped? Was it restored or hot rodded by a future owner? Or is it sitting in a barn somewhere, waiting for you to find it again? If you're daring enough (and crazy enough, as I was) to start looking for it, here's how to do it.

Start by writing down everything you can remember about your car — who sold it to you and when, price paid, condition, how long you owned it, who bought it from you (when and where), and any distinguishing features (dented fender, a non-original steering wheel, etc.) that might help to identify the car when (and if) it turns up.

Round up any and all photos you have of your car. Contact your friends who knew you when you owned it. They might have photos too, and they also might remember details about your car that you may have forgotten.

Phone 1-800-461-3457 and subscribe to *Old Autos*, the twice-monthly newspaper read by forty thousand Canadian hobbyists from coast to coast. Nearly every make of car is represented by a car club devoted to a particular make (e.g. Model A Owners of Canada Inc., with over three hundred members). These clubs are frequently mentioned in *Old Autos*. You can join a club for the make of car you're looking for, you can write a letter to the editor of *Old Autos* to describe your search, or you can contact me (the Old Car Detective) care of *Old Autos* for help in your search.

Visit swap meets (see big listings in *Old Autos*) and look for an original sales catalogue illustrating the car you are looking for. This step will inspire you to keep searching.

Surf the Internet if you have a computer or have access to one. The more people who know what car you're looking for, the greater your chances of finding it.

Finally, if it turns out your first or favourite car was scrapped, don't despair. Find an identical car, phone the owner, and ask if you can go for a ride. Bring your camera along and make some new memories.

CALLING ALL OLD CAR STORIES!

Would you like to see the story of your first car (or favourite car) published in my next book? If so, please send details and laser copies of photos (if available) to:

Bill Sherk, Old Car Detective
c/o *Old Autos*
348 Main Street
Bothwell, Ontario
NOP 1CO